LOST
MISSOURI
TREASURE

W. CRAIG GAINES

THE
History
PRESS

Published by The History Press
Charleston, SC
www.historypress.com

Front cover, top: Missouri Historical Society; *bottom*: State Historical Society of Missouri.
Back cover: Historical Society of Missouri.

First published 2023

Manufactured in the United States

ISBN 978146715014

Library of Congress Control Number: 2023938438

CONTENTS

Introduction

MISSOURI TREASURE

Most of my family is from southeastern Missouri. Many of my ancestors settled in Missouri before the Civil War. From my family I heard tales of the James Gang traveling through southeastern Missouri and hiding out after their robberies. They hid in the swamps, hills and forests near where my family lived. There were also stories of the bloody and destructive Civil War and its aftermath, also part of Missouri history.

This work is derived from my lost treasure research and treasure hunting information I began collecting when I was in junior high school. I spent a lot of time in Missouri, having been born in St. Louis and living in several towns in southeastern and western parts of the state.

These stories range from legends passed down over generations to well-documented historical facts. Where possible, I give my opinion on some of these stories.

Most of Missouri's lost mine stories come from when it was part of the Louisiana Territory under French and Spanish rule. During that time, many expeditions sought gold and silver deposits in the Ozarks, which cover much of southern Missouri. Many areas in the Ozarks had lead, zinc and copper deposits. The Tri-State Mining District covers southwestern Missouri, southeastern Kansas and northeastern Oklahoma. This mining district was a major source of the world's lead and zinc for about a century. The vast deposits gave credibility to the stories of lost Missouri mines.

Missouri became a jumping-off point for traders, migrants, gold seekers and travelers heading west through the American plains and mountains.

St. Louis's Gateway Arch on the Mississippi River marks the starting point of much western frontier travel. *National Park Service*.

Missouri is known as the "Crossroads State" and the "Mother of the West," due to the trails and the Missouri River that travelers used to head west from the eastern United States. Some of these travelers later headed back to their homes with gold and treasure from the West. It was much easier and faster to travel on boats on the Mississippi and Missouri Rivers and their tributaries than traveling over land.

The Santa Fe Trail started in western Missouri, as did the Oregon Trail. St. Louis was a major city, known as the "Gateway to the West." Hostile Indians, outlaws, droughts, storms and disease caused many people to die on these trails. Traveling on steamboats on the Mississippi and Missouri Rivers was often dangerous due to snags and river channel changes, as well as fires, tornadoes, boiler explosions and collisions with other steamboats or low bridges in high water. Hundreds of steamboats lie under the Mississippi and Missouri Rivers and under the ground where these rivers used to meander. Many of these old shipwrecks are now under farmland and wetlands. Some shipwrecks contain valuable cargoes and possibly treasure.

The American Civil War was disastrous for farmers and settlers in southern Missouri. The area became a no-man's-land due to raids from Union and Confederate armies, guerrillas, bushwhackers and outlaws. Before the Civil War, there had been much bloodshed in Southwest Missouri. People's homes were often raided, robbed and burned down. During the war, livestock and crops were often requisitioned or stolen to feed hungry troops who lacked adequate food supplies from their government. A number of towns and villages in mostly Southwest Missouri were sacked, burned down or destroyed in the war. Very few landowners ever received pay for their losses. Many men were murdered and their hidden wealth left in the ground. Banks were often robbed during the Civil War, so people hid their money on their property. Caches were made by guerrillas and bushwhackers who died with their boots on during the war. The Union steamer *Ruth* was set on fire by Confederate saboteurs and sank in the Mississippi River south of Cape Girardeau with a Union army payroll of $2.6 million in greenbacks bound for General Ulysses S. Grant's victorious army, which had captured the Confederate stronghold of Vicksburg, Mississippi. Some of this payroll might remain on or near the *Ruth*.

After the Civil War, outlaws like the James Gang and the James-Younger Gang continued the trade they learned during the war by robbing banks, trains and travelers. Many of these outlaws had ridden with the notorious Colonel William Quantrill and Captain William "Bloody Bill" Anderson. They learned much about robbery during the war. Missouri's James and

Younger families were the source of many outlaws. The state was the home base for many of these notorious outlaws. Tales of loot they left behind involve many places in the state.

Gangsters and criminals continued the tradition of robberies and hidden loot into modern times. St. Louis and Kansas City have several tales of hidden loot. There is still about $300,000 of unaccounted-for paid ransom from the 1953 Greenlease kidnapping.

I sorted through many versions of a number of tales of lost mines, lost treasure and sunken ships to present a logical sequence arranged by county. The values of lost treasures often seem too large for the times. Most Missouri lost mine stories originated before there was a state of Missouri, when the area was mostly unexplored wilderness, at least to the new explorers and migrants. The locations of these lost mines are often vague, due to the time when they were lost. Throughout the text, where sources vary on a fact, I include the variation or variations in parentheses.

Outlaw treasure stories contain conflicting information regarding who the robbers actually were. I used several sources where possible, and these sources often name different outlaws who committed the robberies. Outlaws by nature lie to protect themselves from jail or the noose. And the trials of captured outlaws include conflicts about the robbers' identities. Witnesses often claimed that Jesse and Frank James and their gang members were somewhere else when robberies occurred.

Missouri is also known as the "Cave State" for the thousands of caves in the state. Many of these caves have lost treasure or lost mine stories associated with them.

There were about four hundred steamboat shipwrecks in Missouri and on its borders with Illinois and Kansas. Although the cargoes of many steamboats were salvaged over the years, some ships appear to have never been salvaged or salvaged completely.

I hope you get the chance to roam all over the Show Me State of Missouri and experience its natural wonders and history. These are its greatest treasures.

—W. Craig Gaines
Tulsa, Oklahoma, 2023

1

TREASURES BY COUNTY

Andrew County

Sultan

The side-wheel steamboat *Sultan* sank in 1857 at what became known as Sultan Bend of the Missouri River above Amazonia, Missouri.

Audrain County

Berry's Loot

James Berry was part of the Sam Bass Gang that robbed a train in Big Springs, Nebraska, on September 18, 1877. The gang stole three boxes of newly minted 1877 $20 gold pieces with $20,000 in each box. The Bass Gang also robbed passengers on the train of at least $400. The gang left behind on the train about $200,000 in gold bullion in a safe they could not open, along with silver bullion that was too heavy for them to carry on horseback. While Sam Bass and his gang returned to their stomping grounds in North Texas, James Berry parted company with them and returned to his home in Mexico, Missouri, reportedly with a friend. After James deposited $2,000 in newly minted 1877 $20 gold pieces in the local bank in Mexico, he immediately became a suspect in the Big Springs robbery.

Sheriff Moses Glasscock and detectives from Chicago and St. Louis arrived in Mexico, Missouri, to watch James Berry's movements. Berry did not stay at his family's home but hid elsewhere. The lawmen look Berry's friend Bose Kazey prisoner when Kazey tried to pick up a new suit that Berry had ordered from a local tailor. James Berry rode to Kazey's house to pick up the new suit, but the lawmen were waiting for him. Berry ran away when the lawmen ordered him to surrender. Sheriff Glasscock fired his shotgun and hit Berry in both legs. The lawmen grabbed Berry and recovered $1,840 from him. The injured Berry was carried into Kazey's house. A doctor came to attend to his wounds. James Berry developed gangrene and died on October 18, 1877. He was thought to have hidden money somewhere in the area, but it was never found.

The other members of the Sam Bass Gang in North Texas were chased by lawmen and posses after members of the gang spent the newly minted 1877 $20 gold pieces in stores. The presence of newly minted gold coins was always noted by store clerks and owners. The merchants reported it to lawmen, who reported it to railroad and other detectives. Posses were quickly formed to hunt down the Bass Gang. The gang had a number of gunfights before they managed to escape the law. In need of money that had not been newly minted, the Bass Gang rode to southern Texas and tried to rob a Round Rock bank on July 20, 1878. One gang member had alerted the law about the robbery, so several lawmen ambushed the gang at Round Rock. A deputy sheriff and an outlaw were killed in the shootout. Sam Bass was severely wounded and died the next day, his twenty-fifth birthday.

Barry County

Indian Eagle Rock Mine and Cave

On Turkey Mountain, Indians reportedly had several mines. They may have hidden silver bullion in a cave near Eagle Rock that they sealed off when they left the region. This is in the same area as the White River Mines.

Indian Silver Mine

An Indian silver mine was said to be located in the southeastern part of the county near Easley Ford on the White River.

Lost Chickasaw Mine

Some Chickasaw Indians reportedly had a mine after they were relocated to Missouri and Arkansas before being pushed into Indian Territory. As white settlers came into the area, the Chickasaws hid the mine entrance with rocks. It was said to be near Exeter.

Lock Treasure

John (Jonas) Lock was said to have owned a tavern, farm and racetrack in the 1840s. When he died, his estate had just $7,000 in assets. Many people thought he had hidden money on his farm, as he was considered a very wealthy man for those times.

Rockhouse Cave Treasure

A Cuban appeared in Barry County in 1936 looking for what turned out to be Rockhouse Cave. This cave was located between Shell Knob and Cassville. The entrance to Rockhouse Cave was below a cliff in Rockhouse Valley. The Cuban spent several days hunting for the treasure based on a map he had. The story was that a group of Spaniards with Aztec gold were traveling through present-day Barry County when they were attacked by hostile Indians. Only one Spaniard escaped the massacre, hiding in a cave. The Indians did not take the Spaniards' gold bullion, so the surviving Spaniard moved the gold to a cave or some other place and left the area. The Spaniard sailed to Cuba with a map of the hidden treasure location, which was later obtained by the Cuban, who searched for the treasure.

Sugar Silver Cave

Sugar Silver Cave is near Big Sugar Creek, not far from the Missouri-Arkansas line in Mark Twain National Forest. This was a commercial cave leased by the Tate brothers for many years. The cave was big enough to walk into and extended six hundred feet into the side of a hill. It was rumored to contain treasure. Parts of the cave were dynamited in the search for loot.

The cave was deemed unsafe due to the dynamite damage, which affected the cave's stability. The cave was closed.

WHITE RIVER MINES

About 1800, a Frenchman with an Indian (black man) departed St. Louis. They traveled about eight days to the southwest. They reportedly discovered a mine (cave) with human bones and a six-foot-wide vein of silver inside. After mining much silver and fearing Indian attacks, they hid the mine entrance and made a map of the mine's location. The two men headed back toward St. Louis. One partner was killed by hostile Indians. The other partner took the map and compiled a diary of the trip. He, too, was later killed. One version has them leaving silver bullion in the cave.

Pu Deville and Pierre somehow ended up with the map and diary. Dr. Smith of St. Louis (St. Charles) and a man named LeDuc grubstaked Pu Deville and Pierre to look for the lost mine. Pu Deville and Pierre reportedly found the mine and silver bars there. They hid the entrance and drew their own map. They wrote in their diaries about the stacks of silver bullion and mining tools in the mine.

Hostile Indians killed Pu Deville and Pierre after they left the mine. Indians and Spaniards were said to have mined silver from the site at a later date. In 1830, the map and two diaries detailing the mine's location were discovered in St. Louis in a gun barrel. A Choctaw Indian reportedly also drew a map to the mine. People who saw the map thought the mine was located near the White River near Easley Ford in southeast Barry County. Ola Farwell of Eureka Springs, Arkansas, ended up with the maps and diaries. Several people used this information to write articles about the lost mine site.

Table Rock Dam was built in 1959 and may have inundated the lost mine. One diary had information about a creek coming out of a rock cliff with a lot of noise (roaring river). The tributary went into another creek, then into a river. A diary indicated that the prospectors traveled six to eight miles to a little valley running south and a narrow ravine between two high bluffs, which was where the mine was located. Based on the map, Murphy and Kietz owned the land where the mine was believed to be hidden. In 1940, they sold their land on the White River and the map they had acquired to brothers Ola and Audrey Farwell. The Farwells hunted for the mine but never found it. The lost mine might be elsewhere. It is possible that this was a lead mine and not a silver mine.

BARTON COUNTY

TIN WHISTLE LOOT

In the 1930s, a bootlegger and a couple of his outlaw friends held up a farm close to Arcadia, Kansas, taking jewelry, gold, weapons and photos. They drove to Kansas City and buried the loot north of Milford. It was said to be hidden in a small cave close to Horse Creek. This story was posted on the Legends of America website by a man who heard the story from his bootlegger grandfather, who died in 1997 in Tulsa, Oklahoma.

BATES COUNTY

WHITE OAK HILL GUERRILLA GOLD

During the Civil War, a Confederate guerrilla band reportedly robbed a bank near Adrian and stole $90,000 worth of gold. Union soldiers chased the band, which may have cached three buckskin bags of gold at the base of a large tree about eight miles west of Adrian. A legend says that White Oak Hill was the burial location. Union troops chased the guerrillas into Kansas, where the band was caught and all of its members killed. One guerrilla supposedly revealed the gold's location before he died.

BENTON COUNTY

MIGRATING INDIANS CACHE

In the 1830s, Indians living in the southeastern United States were traveling on routes that became known as the Trail of Tears to present-day Oklahoma. Along one route, a group of Indians reportedly buried valuables, money and jewelry near Warsaw. Some versions of this story claimed the cache contained renegade Indian loot consisting of stolen jewels, gold and silver. The Lake of the Ozarks near Warsaw may now cover a cave and its treasure cache. In one tale, a posse reportedly killed all the renegade Indians. Another version has the Indians migrating out of this area and leaving the treasure behind.

Bollinger County

See "Bollinger Treasure," Cape Girardeau County.

Boone County

Kaffer Treasure Cache

Near Armstrong, a cache of gold coins was reportedly hidden about forty miles northwest of Columbia.

Butler County

Found Treasure Chest

In 1972, my cousin Adam Frank Smith was told a story about one of his relatives finding a treasure chest. Adam's uncle, Basil Dean Smith, said that his Grandpa Burlison discovered a cave along the St. Francis River near Fisk. The river is the dividing line between Butler and Stoddard Counties. Investigating the cave, Grandpa Burlison found a chest with deerskin bags of gold and silver coins that were likely French or Spanish. Due to its weight, he was unable to carry all of the treasure out of the cave at once. He likely had to make another trip to get the rest of the loot. The Burlison family owned much land in Stoddard County and reportedly lost more than $100,000 in a failed Puxico bank during the Great Depression. Part of the family's wealth may have come from proceeds of this treasure. This treasure might have been found in the 1890s or the first decade of the 1900s, when there was a lot of activity converting swamps to farmland by draining them and cutting down forests. It is possible the cave was in Stoddard County; it is more likely that it was in the uplands south of present-day Lake Wappapello.

CALDWELL COUNTY

WINSTON RAILROAD ROBBERY LOOT

See Daviess County.

CALLAWAY COUNTY

E.A. OGDEN

See Cole County.

MOLLIE DOZZIER

While carrying gold miners and treasure from the gold fields, the side-wheeler *Mollie Dozzier* was snagged near Council Bluffs, Nebraska, and sank. The vessel was quickly refloated, but many of the passengers with their gold decided not to continue downstream on the Missouri River. On October 1, 1866 (sources vary about the exact date), opposite Chamois, Missouri, the *Mollie Dozzier* hit another snag, and several miners reportedly died because

This steamboat wreck was one of hundreds on the Missouri River. *State Historical Society of Missouri.*

of the weight of gold they were carrying (possibly in their money belts). Captain Fred Dozzier was the ship's owner and master. The wreck is located in what is known as Mollie Dozzier Chute. There are rumors of gold still being aboard.

This likely is the same 384-ton *Mollie Dozzier* that was built in 1865 and reportedly snagged on October 3, 1866 (the date varies), at Plattsmouth, Nebraska, on the Missouri River. It is likely that the steamboat was raised and later sank near Chamois. During a survey of the Missouri River by the U.S. Army Corps of Engineers in 1868, it was noted that the *Mollie Dozzier* (*Dozier*) sank in the channel at Alert Bend.

Timour No. 2

See Cole County.

Camden County

Lost Missouri Mine

See Dallas County.

Cape Girardeau County

Benton Hill Treasure

Former slave George Bollinger told a story about spirits guarding hidden gold close to a peach orchard near Benton Hill. This story appeared as part of the Federal Writers' Project compilation *Slave Narratives*, volume 10.

Bollinger Treasure

The Bollinger family hid a three-foot-long chest containing gold and silver in their attic under rugs before the Civil War, according to George Bollinger, who had been a slave for the family. When the Civil War began, the treasure chest was removed by several men and buried near the Bollinger family cemetery, not far from a "sugar grove"—likely an orchard or group of trees. During the war, soldiers from both sides often came to the Bollinger Plantation. One party of Confederate troops reportedly stopped at the plantation, where Mrs. Bollinger let them have a large cow and corn from their ten corncribs. News that a Union force was nearby caused the Confederates to leave.

One day, a group of bushwhackers invaded the Bollinger Plantation after hearing there was gold hidden there. To force old man Bollinger to disclose the treasure's location, the bushwhackers strung him up with a rope tied around his neck. He refused to tell them its location, so they murdered him. Afterward, people searched for the treasure, but there is no report of anyone finding it.

It is likely the Bollinger family in this story were among the Germans who settled in Southeast Missouri under the leadership of George Frederick Bollinger. He brought twenty families of settlers to this area in 1799. They settled in what is now Bollinger County and Cape Girardeau County. Among the settlers were George Frederick's brothers John and Daniel, along with Mathias Bollinger and nephews Marion Henry Bell and William Bollinger.

The Bollingers had several mills in the area. Today, the Bollinger Mill State Historic Site is at Bufordville on the Whitewater River. The first mill at

This Bollinger Mill may be near where the Bollinger treasure was hidden during the Civil War. *Author collection.*

this site was built by George Frederick Bollinger in 1800 and was modified in 1825. He died in 1842. The mill was run by the Bollinger family. A Union scouting party consisting of Company F, Twelfth Missouri Cavalry Regiment fought skirmishes at and near Daniel Bollinger's mill on July 28, 1863, reportedly killing ten to fifteen Confederate soldiers without losing any men. This mill was burned down during the war. A four-story mill was erected on the site in 1867 and is still standing, with modifications having been made over time.

The Bollinger Plantation was in Bollinger County or Cape Girardeau County. Another Bollinger mill, Dollie's Mill, was in Bollinger County on Big Whitewater Creek. It was erected about 1800 by Urban Asher Brenner and Barbera Bollinger on land owned by the Bollinger family. This mill burned down several times, with its last destruction in 1897.

George Bollinger told this story of lost Bollinger treasure around 1935, when he was eighty-four. It appeared as part of the Federal Writers' Project compilation *Slave Narratives*, volume 10.

BRYCE ESTATE TREASURE

The Bryce Estate was located near Cape Girardeau along the Mississippi River. Reportedly, A.C. Shank recovered a $30,000 cache from the estate. More unfound treasure was supposedly hidden on the estate.

SPANISH TREASURE CAVE

This cave is three hundred feet long and has a legend of Spanish treasure associated with it.

CARROLL COUNTY

WILLIAM BAIRD

See Lafayette County.

CASS COUNTY

COLE YOUNGER CACHE

Outlaw Cole Younger likely hid several caches of loot from his robberies. *Library of Congress.*

Thomas Coleman Younger, who was called Cole Younger, was a member of the notorious James-Younger Gang of robbers. Cole grew up on his father Colonel Henry Washington Younger's farm near Harrisonville, which Henry had purchased in 1858. The Youngers were farmers with cattle and later moved into Harrisonville, where Colonel Younger had businesses, including a livery stable. Colonel Younger was murdered on July 20, 1862, while returning home from Kansas City (Westport) carrying $1,500. The family moved from Harrisonville to the country. During the Civil War, the Younger family homes were burned down. Cole was a Confederate captain. After the war, he and his brothers Jim, John and Bob were outlaws in the James-Younger Gang. Some speculate that Cole buried treasure in the Harrisonville area. Others contend he didn't bury any money. On September 21, 1876, Cole, Bob and Jim Younger were captured after the Northfield, Minnesota bank robbery fiasco. Cole Younger was imprisoned for many years. After being released, he held various jobs, including working as an attraction in a Wild West show with Frank James.

POCAHONTAS NO. 2

The side-wheel steamer *Pocahontas No. 2* carried a cargo consisting mostly of grain. It was snagged one-half mile below Rock Bluff (Rock Bluffs) on August 11, 1840, while heading down the Missouri River. Its hull was ripped open from stem to stern, and the vessel immediately sank. The boat's cabin furniture, books and money were saved.

SPANISH MINERS TREASURE

Robert Tatham's book *Missouri Treasures and Civil War Sites* has a story about a lost treasure that was mentioned in the October 24, 1879 edition of the

Cass County Times Courier. It is a tale from a Spaniard named Crow who gave A.I. (the initials of the letter writer) the story in 1838 about 1,000 Spaniards who left New Orleans in February 1772 to mine in northern Texas and other Spanish-owned areas at that time. After mining for a period and having many battles with Indians, their numbers were reduced to about 750. They decided to return to New Orleans with their gold. Their large caravan was continually attacked by ever-increasing numbers of hostile Indians at the end of October 1772. They reportedly buried gold about 240 to 300 yards southeast of a spring in a ravine and covered it with loose rock to a depth of three feet with dirt piled on top. The silver was buried about three-fourths of a mile from the gold burial place. The treasure was supposed to be fifteen mule loads with a weight of 130 pounds for each load. There were one thousand 20-pound silver bars. The Indian attacks continued; finally, only Crow and Don Carlos from the Spanish party were alive. The two returned to Spain, where Don Carlos died. Crow returned to America to recover the treasure in 1853. He was ill and told the letter writer (A.I.) about the treasure location. A.I. believed the treasure was about one-quarter mile from the Rodman Schoolhouse, which was four to five miles west and one to one and a half miles north of Harrisonville. It is likely that this is a tall tale written for entertainment in a small newspaper. People have looked for the treasure in the area using bulldozers and other equipment. Many people seem to have searched for this treasure over the years, but there has been no report of anyone finding the loot. I personally think the account is fiction. But who knows?

Cedar County

Church Hollow Treasure

Church Hollow was a small rural community with a church, a mill and a few houses located in a hollow with Cedar Creek to the west and the Sac River to the east. In the early part of the Civil War, three friends from the Church Hollow community joined the Confederate army. Before they left the area, they reportedly pooled their money and put it in a large kettle. The kettle was so heavy that two men had to carry and cache it. A rough map of the kettle was carved on a rock, and several symbols were carved on nearby rocks to help locate the cache.

On August 10, 1861, at the Battle of Wilson's Creek, just southwest of Springfield, Missouri, one of the three friends was killed. Another of the friends died a few days later. The lone survivor returned to Church Hollow, but his mind was so affected by the war that his recollections of the past were hazy and fragmented. His friends helped him search for the kettle of money, but it was never located. He said the kettle was "30 minutes east of the church."

In 1960, St. Clair Historical Society members Dr. John J. Sullivan and James D. Atteberry surveyed the site of Church Hollow when a new dam was being planned for the area. Two of the markers believed to have been left by the Confederate soldiers were found on Cedar Bluff. The image of a kettle on one of the carvings resembled the topography of the area. It has been surmised that "30 minutes east of the church" was really a compass bearing rather than a walking distance. No one has reported finding this cache.

LOST CARPENTER CREEK GOLD MINE

This lost gold mine was said to be near Jerico Springs.

The Battle of Wilson's Creek affected three young Confederate soldiers. Their Church Hollow Treasure is still lost. *Library of Congress.*

CHRISTIAN COUNTY

HOAX SPANISH MYSTERY STONE

See Greene County.

LOST SPANISH TREASURE

According to lore, a lost Spanish treasure consisting of several mule loads of silver was hidden by a mining party near Pineville. The legend claimed it was near an old Spanish cave south of Ozark on a high knoll overlooking a winding stream in a valley.

SPANISH PERUVIAN TREASURE AND LOST MINE

See Douglas County.

CLARION COUNTY

MISSOURI RIVER LOST KETTLE OF FRENCH GOLD

In October 1802, four Frenchmen rowed upstream of the Missouri River in a boat from St. Louis with a cargo of trading goods and a copper kettle full of French gold coins for a French trading post to the west. After several days, they camped on the north side of the Missouri River below low bluffs. A band of Indians attacked them, so they held them off behind makeshift barricades and were trapped. After several days of battle in the cold, three of the Frenchmen died. One man was seriously injured but made his way to their boat and floated downstream. He reached St. Louis and told his story of the lost gold. He then died.

W.C. Jameson's book *Lost Mines and Buried Treasures of Missouri* details that in 1935 an old Indian woman came looking for the lost French treasure. She had a 1795 French coin and claimed it was from one of her ancestors who had attacked the Frenchmen. In the 1930s, a skeleton and a French copper disk were found at a site under construction at the base of bluffs near where the Missouri and Grand Rivers meet near New Brunswick. It was thought the skeleton was that of a French trader.

A farmer was plowing his field in 1941 and noticed a reflection in the field within thirty yards of a slight limestone bluff. After examining it, he found that the reflection was a 1795 French gold coin. He and others looked for more but found none, it appears. This coin may have been part of the lost kettle of French gold treasure.

CLAY COUNTY

LIBERTY BANK ROBBERY LOOT

On February 13, 1866, approximately twelve men rode into the town of Liberty. It is likely that all or almost all of them were former members of William Quantrill's guerrilla band. While several (or most) of them waited in the street in front of the Clay County Savings Association Building, most of the others (two) went inside. The father and son who ran the bank were ordered by the outlaws to fill a large wheat sack with valuables. Between $60,000 and $70,000 in gold and silver coins, currency, bonds, certificates and stamps to cash the certificates ($72,000 in coins and currency) were taken. Frank Triplett's book *The Life, Times & Treacherous Death of Jesse James* claims that only $2,000 was taken. Private funds of gold

Outlaw Frank James supposedly hid a number of caches of loot in Missouri and other states. *Missouri Historical Society.*

and silver in three bags were also stolen. One bystander, seventeen-year-old (or twelve-year-old) student George Wymore, was killed outside the bank. Wymore attended William Jewell College in Liberty. Some robbers wore blue army overcoats. All of the robbers were thought to be former Confederate guerrillas. The robbery caused the bank to fail and go out of business.

Arch Clement, who rode with William Quantrill and Bloody Bill Anderson during the Civil War, was likely a member of the gang. Some believe that Jesse James was also part of this robbery, but others claim he was sick in bed at the time. Jesse's brother Frank James was in Kentucky and not a part of the gang robbing the bank. Cole Younger might have been one of the robbers. The outlaw gang rode to Mount Gilead Church, where they divided the loot and then went in different directions. The gang members were said to have crossed the Missouri River on a ferry. A posse was formed but was slowed down by a storm. The bank was reportedly owned by former Union officers and had been a target of the former rebels. This was believed to be the first U.S. bank robbery after the Civil War. Some people claimed that loot from the robbery was hidden nearby.

According to a variation of this story, one robber carried most of the loot and hid it before rendezvousing with the gang. The gang killed him when he would not tell them where he cached the loot. Arch Clement was shot and killed by Missouri State Militia after interfering with an election in 1866 at Lexington, Missouri. The bank building today houses the Jesse James Bank Museum.

TWILIGHT

The *Twilight*, a 230-ton, 180-foot-long, 32-foot-wide side-wheeler, was sunk by a snag on September 10, 1865, east of Missouri City. It was said to have sunk opposite the mouth of Fire Creek, one-half to one-quarter mile above Napoleon. The *Twilight* was heavily loaded with a cargo of gin, weapons, military uniforms and other supplies bound for the mountain trade. No lives were lost in its sinking. Many parties over the years salvaged much of its cargo. A salvage in 1895 does not appear to have recovered much, but another in 1897 recovered much of the cargo. The hull was drilled through, but no indications were found of remaining cargo. In 2001, the wreck site was dewatered with twenty wells, and about ninety thousand cubic yards of earth and material were removed during the excavation. The *Twilight*'s hull, two steam engines, paddle wheels and various remaining cargo were removed.

CLINTON COUNTY

WINSTON RAILROAD ROBBERY LOOT

See Daviess County.

Missouri's capital, Jefferson City, had several steamboats wrecked nearby in the Missouri River. *Missouri Historical Society.*

COLE COUNTY

E.A. OGDEN

The 399-ton *E.A. Ogden* was built in 1855 and snagged on February 22, 1860, near Jefferson City while carrying military supplies and possibly a gold shipment bound for Fort Leavenworth. No lives were lost when it sank.

TIMOUR NO. 2

The 232-ton side-wheel steamer *Timour No. 2* was built in 1849. Three miles below Jefferson City on the Missouri River, its boilers exploded on August 21, 1854, near the right bank one mile above the Moreau River. Between thirty and forty (seventeen by one report) people were killed, including the master, pilot and clerk. The ship's safe was blown onto a nearby bluff and recovered. The shipwreck was visible in the water in the 1890s. This shipwreck could be in Callaway County.

COOPER COUNTY

GEORGE WASHINGTON

The 355-ton side-wheel steamer *George Washington* was probably built in 1825. While carrying U.S. government stores of firearms and a possible shipment of gold to Fort Calhoun / Council Bluffs, Iowa, it sank at Hardemans Orchard opposite the LaMine River. It may have been raised, as the steamer *George Washington* was burned in 1831 at New Orleans, Louisiana.

RADNER

The 165-ton side-wheel *Radner* was built in 1844. The *Radner* carried about 60 tons of U.S. government stores bound for Fort Leavenworth. The vessel sank just above the mouth of the LaMine River on July 28, 1846, with no lives lost. Both cargo and vessel were a total loss.

CRAWFORD COUNTY

ELLIS TRUST CACHE

In 1925, Ellis Trust was a farmworker in Louisiana who slept in a barn. One day, he was awakened by gunshots and the sound of horses. He watched as outlaws came into the barn and buried gold. The outlaws covered the burial place with hay before they fled. Trust reportedly dug up enough gold to fill a one-gallon bucket. He carried the bucket of gold as he headed toward his home in Huzzah, Missouri. It was an arduous trip, and he came down sick. Finally, he could carry the gold no farther, so he buried it a few miles (three miles) from Huzzah. By the time he reached his home, he had a bad case of pneumonia. Before dying, Trust told his brother that there was a spring he had drunk from near Huzzah. He said that he then traveled up a small hollow from the spring to a shelter rock (rock shelter), where he discovered a foxhole under the bluff. He put the gold in the foxhole and covered the entrance with rocks. He found a horse's skull and put it under the shelter rock as a marker. This cache was said to be near Haunted Springs up a hollow.

Dallas County

Lost Missouri Mine

A legend held that during the Civil War, Confederates sealed off a silver mine to prevent Union troops from mining it. The lost mine was reportedly near Louisburg. It may be in Camden, Hickory or Polk Counties.

Meramec River Treasure

See Franklin County.

Daviess County

Winston Railroad Robbery Loot

The Chicago, Rock Island & Pacific Railroad was robbed on the night of July 15, 1881, by between four and seven masked robbers as it left Winston. One report claimed that Jesse James, Frank James, Dick Liddil, Clarence Hite and Wood Hite were the robbers, but other men were also said to have been the robbers. The outlaws stopped the train and robbed the baggage car. Conductor William Westfall was murdered, even though he had raised his hands to surrender to the outlaws. Westfall was shot in the back. Train passenger John McCulloch (Frank McMillan) was also shot and killed. Westfall may have been murdered for his involvement in transporting detectives to Clay County in January 1875. These detectives set off the bomb that killed Frank and Jesse James's half brother Archie and severely crippled their mother. There also was a detective with the last name of Westfall who was involved in persecuting members of the James Gang, so there may be more to this story than what has been told.

A member of the gang hit messenger Charles Murray in the baggage car to get him to hand over the keys to the safe. The safe was opened, and the robbers reportedly stole between $8,000 and $15,000 from the baggage car (express car). The robbers' horses were near where the train was stopped on the siding near Winston. The robbers cut the leashes that tied the horses to trees and then rode away. The gang reportedly rode around Cameron and then to the Missouri River, where some may have crossed the river.

Some believed that the robbery was the work of Jesse and Frank James and their gang. The law claimed that Frank James murdered William Westfall. Frank was later brought to trial on this robbery but was acquitted after conflicting evidence was presented. Some of the loot may have been stashed near Winston. Any cached loot could be in Caldwell, Clinton or DeKalb Counties.

DEKALB COUNTY

WINSTON RAILROAD ROBBERY LOOT

See Daviess County.

DENT COUNTY

MONEY CAVE

This cave was probably named for a treasure story. It is nine hundred feet long and has a twenty-one-foot stream fall as well as upper levels.

DOUGLAS COUNTY

SPANISH PERUVIAN TREASURE AND LOST MINE

Before 1800, Spanish ships with Peruvian treasure supposedly went up the lower Mississippi River and were chased by French ships. The Spaniards reportedly sailed upriver to shallow water that the French ships could not navigate. The Spaniards left their ships and searched for gold in the Ozarks. They went by land and found a rich mine. Their Peruvian treasure was said to have been stored in the mine. When Napoleon Bonaparte sold Louisiana to the United States in the Louisiana Purchase, the Spaniards hid their mine and left the area. It was thought they were either killed by hostile Indians or died in shipwrecks. In the early 1930s, a mine entrance was said to have been discovered and lost again. Beaver Creek reportedly flooded the mine. The mine might be in Christian, Ozark or Taney Counties. This story is similar to that of the lost Louisiana Mine in Franklin County, Arkansas.

Several treasures were reportedly hidden along the Meramec River. *Missouri Historical Society.*

FRANKLIN COUNTY

MERAMEC RIVER TREASURE

Along the Meramec River south of Stanton, legends indicated that loot from guerrilla raids and bank robberies during the Civil War were buried in or near the 6,896-acre Meramec State Park.

GASCONADE COUNTY

BIG HATCHEE TREASURE

The stern-wheel steamboat *Big Hatchee* sank on July 25, 1845 (1843) at Hermann in the Missouri River after its boiler exploded. The steamer was carrying about one hundred German immigrants to Omaha, along with a reported cargo of mercury and whiskey. The death toll is unknown, but forty of the immigrants were buried in unmarked graves in the Hermann Cemetery. The reported mercury cargo is suspect, since gold was not mined in Montana until 1858. This story derives in part from a *Saga* magazine article.

FOUND COINS

After the Missouri River flood in the spring of 1973, the U.S. Army Corps of Engineers was repairing damaged levees when one of its contract workers found an old Spanish coin that had been dredged up out of the river. Ray Volker and Dick Richmond's book *Treasure under Your Feet* documents the search that followed the find. Volker and the worker found more Spanish and U.S. coins dated between 1790 and 1820 and a gold stickpin. The coins were found in the area that was using dredge material to rebuild the levee. Volker did research and thought the coins were part of the treasure from the three-hundred-ton side-wheel steamer *Boreas No. 2*, which had been powered by two engines and was built in 1845 or 1846. A picture in Volker and Richmond's book shows eleven and three-fourths coins (two were half coins and one was a one-quarter coin that had been cut). The *Boreas No. 2* sank in 1846 and was reported as carrying "a large amount of silver money onboard. The steamboat supposed to have been set on fire and the money stolen." Volker didn't give the exact location of the treasure find but indicated that it was near Hermann. It could be in Franklin, Montgomery or Warner Counties.

GREENE COUNTY

HOAX SPANISH MYSTERY STONE TREASURE

On November 17, 1965, Cub Scouts found a sandstone slab with a Spanish inscription in the southeast area of Wilson's Creek National Battlefield Park. It was found where an old road crossed Wilson's Creek. According to the Spanish inscription on the stone, eight Spaniards transporting gold and silver left Ysleto Pueblo in what is now New Mexico bound for St. Louis. On June 4, 1799, the Spaniards met a group of French and Americans, so they hid their gold and silver in a cave. The Spanish mystery stone was exhibited in the park for a while. Several professors were said to have determined that the stone markings were genuine. I saw the stone when I was much younger, when the park was being developed and there was only a trailer for the park's headquarters before the visitor center was built. It was later discovered that the stone was a hoax carved by a local man as a joke. This story of Spanish treasure seems to have been based on a local legend that the Spanish had mined silver and hid three kegs of gold in the mine.

LOST SPANISH AND FRENCH MINES

The French and Spanish supposedly had several lost silver mines and gold mines near Springfield. An 1858 letter written in Spanish reportedly on buckskin was translated and published in the July 1935 edition of the *Springfield News and Leader*. Roy Preacher, an early Springfield settler, reportedly had this letter. Preacher died in 1865, and the letter ended up being passed down in his family.

The letter was dated May 10, 1858, from Delverte, Mexico. It gave detailed instructions on how to find a hidden room in a cave with three kegs of gold. First it said to go to the southwest corner of the square in Springfield, Missouri, in Greene County. Then, it instructed the reader to follow an old road through the square, southwest about two and a half miles to an east–west road and then go west about one-half mile to a large spring with several cabins and trees. There were sinkholes or pits about four hundred steps southwest of the large spring, and there was a bluff across the creek. The directions were a little confusing, as they directed going down the creek three hundred steps to another spring. About midway in the bluff was the primary entrance to a cave. The cave entrance was blocked with a large stone with three turkey tracks running east to west on the stone. Behind the stone, the cave was filled for twelve to thirteen feet. The reader was to go down a passage about twelve feet to a south passage and then down a southeast passage into a large room. This room was where the Spanish smelted bullion into Spanish coins. The writer claimed that his father and brother had worked there. More directions were given from three oak trees cut with one turkey track in one tree, two turkey tracks in another tree and two turkey tracks in a third tree.

This letter is likely a hoax, based on the descriptions, as far as I can see. There was another letter written in the 1890s with similar directions but using slightly different wording.

Robert H. Gibbons's article "Lost Spanish Gold in a Missouri Cave" was published in *Treasure World* magazine. He did a lot of investigation in the Springfield area regarding this tale. He believed the road from the Springfield square was the Old Wire Road, which was named after the telegraph line that ran along this early road. He identified the two springs as being near Sunshine Street and Scenic Drive, near where the Jordan River forks into Wilson's Creek near a bluff. The Missouri Pacific Railroad was later built at the location identified in the letter as being where the cave or mine entrance was located. A stone quarry was later placed at this site, and much limestone rock was removed. Perhaps the quarry owners were looking for the lost mine and treasure by excavating away the rock. Maybe they found what they were looking for.

A similar letter was owned by Colonel John W. Lizenby. It gave similar directions to a Spanish treasure but was reportedly written on July 24, 1893, by F.F. Fritz from Mason, Michigan, and was sent to C.B. Littlefield in Knob Noster, Missouri.

In the 1930s, two men were said to have directions to a cave in a letter in their possession. The men reportedly found the cave. They failed to find any Spanish treasure despite searching several parts of the cave, with one part about one hundred feet below the other. W.C. Jameson's Missouri treasure book also has similar instructions and history.

NOBLE HILL TREASURE

See Polk County.

HICKORY COUNTY

LOST BROOKSIE SILVER MINE

The Lost Brooksie Silver Mine was reportedly near the town of Cross Timbers. This was supposedly a silver mine that existed before the Civil War. Union troops entered the area, so the Confederates dammed the Pomme de Terre River to flood and hide the mine. This mine site may be underwater, as three miles southwest of Cross Timbers is the southeast corner of Lake of the Ozarks.

LOST MISSOURI MINES

See Dallas County.

HOLT COUNTY

REVEREND TOBIAS'S LOST SATCHEL

Circuit-riding preacher J.H. Tobias was crossing rain-swollen Squaw Creek at a ford near Ross Grove on June 18, 1884, when his buggy turned over in the water. His buggy team drowned. Reverend Tobias's satchel, containing his life savings and papers, was lost in the creek. It was thought that he had been headed to Ross Grove. The local people he served gave him another buggy and team, but his money was reportedly lost and never found. Some stories put his lost savings at about $150 in gold.

SULTANNA TREASURE

The steamboat *Sultanna* (*Sultana*) sank about two miles south of Big Lake in the Missouri River with a rumored treasure of $65,000 in gold coins. I did not find this ship among the shipwreck lists, so it could be a phantom vessel that never existed.

W.R. CARUTHERS TREASURE

The steamer *W.R. Caruthers* was said to have carried $30,000 in gold coins when it sank in the east side of the Missouri River near Big Lake, about ten miles west of Mound City. The author did not find this ship among the shipwrecks lists, so it could be a phantom ship that never existed.

HOWARD COUNTY

CHARITON

The 112-ton side-wheel, single-engine steamer *Chariton* was built in 1835. The vessel, 160 feet long and 25 feet wide, became snagged below Glasgow in Eurphrate Bend in the Missouri River as it was heading for Independence. No lives were lost when it sank. Some cargo was saved, along with a large amount of U.S. government money. It had previously sank and been raised at the mouth of the Gasconade River on the Missouri

Missouri River snags sank many steamboats. Some might still contain cargo and treasure. *Missouri Historical Society.*

River. It had been repaired and put back into service before its October 1836 sinking below Glasgow.

GEORGE WASHINGTON

See Cooper County.

KAFFER TREASURE

The Kaffer treasure of gold coins was said to be near Armstrong.

RADENER

See Cooper County.

HOWELL COUNTY

BUSHWHACKER'S LOOT

In January 1863, Confederate Colonel Joseph C. Porter led nine hundred troops from Pocahontas, Arkansas, into Missouri on a raid. A party of four bushwhackers rode ahead of the invading Confederate column. The four men looted homes and robbed people in Franklin, Whites Haws and Pilot Hill. At Sturkie, Arkansas, they reportedly stole $900 in loot. The bushwhackers gathered several mule loads of loot, including three thousand pieces of silverware, jewelry, thirty pocket watches, 470 silver dollars and $9,000 in gold eagles and double eagles. This cache totaled $13,000, according to one version of the story.

One of the bushwhackers, Henry Williams (Hanford Croce in other versions; could be both, as one might have been an alias), was wearing a Union uniform. About four miles north of Sturkie, Arkansas, in Missouri (but may be in Arkansas), the four bushwhackers stopped at a spring. The sound of a barking dog alerted them, and they spotted four Confederate soldiers heading their way. The bushwhackers decided to cache their loot in a sinkhole about four hundred yards from the spring. On the northwest edge of the sinkhole, they either dug a hole or put the loot in a small cave.

The four Confederate soldiers captured the four bushwhackers. Suddenly, about a dozen Union soldiers attacked the Confederates and the bushwhackers. Two Confederate soldiers were killed in the attack. The Union soldiers then hanged the remaining two Confederate soldiers and three of the bushwhackers. Henry Williams was in a Union uniform, so he claimed he had been captured by the Confederates. Williams gave the Union soldiers information on Colonel Porter's Confederate forces, so the Union soldiers returned Williams's horse, and he was taken to West Plains. The Black family, the Kellam family and others helped Williams move to Rolla. He later went to Knobview and St. Louis. Williams joined a Union Illinois regiment and guarded the Evansville, Indiana riverfront during the Civil War.

Henry Williams was unable to return to recover the bushwhackers' treasure, but on his deathbed at a Kansas City hospital at age seventy-seven in 1912 (1911), he told the story of the lost treasure to another patient, Tom Hoots. Hoots moved to West Plains and questioned members of the Black and Kellam families about Henry Williams. None of these family members remembered Henry.

Tom Hoots moved to Archie, Missouri, near Kansas City. Hoot's son remained in West Plains. In 1935, while looking for a recently fallen meteorite, the younger Hoots found a sinkhole, spring and grove of trees where he believed the two Confederates and three bushwhackers had been hanged, according to the story his father had relayed to him. Hoots and three of his friends spent five days digging and looking for the treasure.

They found two pieces of silverware and a rusted hunting knife but no other treasure. In 1972, a member of the Hoots family detailed the story of their ancestor and this treasure in a *Treasure World* article.

CHARLES BOUCHER CACHE

Charles Boucher was a French trapper who had a successful trapping season. He took his furs to Cape Girardeau in 1902 and sold them for about four hundred silver dollars. While heading home, he noticed two strangers following him at a distance. He rode for several days with the two strangers still following. He crossed the Eleven Point River and finally arrived at his home. He told his family that he was being followed, so he reportedly cached his $400 ($500) in silver coins near his cabin and ponds south of West Plains and left. His family never saw him again. It was thought the two strangers attacked and killed him for the money they thought he was carrying.

COLONEL PORTER'S TREASURE

Confederate Colonel Joseph C. Porter and his soldiers supposedly hid $30,000 in gold and silver coins near Lanton, on the Missouri-Arkansas border. Colonel Porter was wounded by cannon fire during an attack on Union troops at the Battle of Hartville in Wright County. Porter died on February 18, 1863, at Batesville, Arkansas. This could be a version of "Bushwhacker's Loot."

SINKHOLE TREASURE

In a sinkhole on a farm near Hocomo, about $35,000 in gold and silver coins were said to have been hidden. The sinkhole was reportedly flooded to further hide the treasure.

Jackson County

Bone Hill Treasure

A farmer and his family lived on Bone Hill with their slaves before the Civil War. Bone Hill got its name from buffalo bones scattered on the hill. These bones were likely left over from an Indian camp where buffalo were butchered. A stone wall was built across the family's farm. The farm was sold in 1862, during the war. Before leaving his property, the farmer reportedly buried his gold savings. The farmer and his family were said to have wanted to return in seven years to recover their treasure.

A ghost light was reported on the hill in 1869 and was said to show up every seven years thereafter. Some people thought it was the spirit of the dead farmer looking for his gold in the Bone Hill Cemetery. The cache site was said to be near the old stone wall, about one and a half miles south of Levasy on the west side of H Highway.

Chavez Owens Landing Treasure

Mexican Don Antonio José Chavez left Santa Fe with two wagons, about fifty-five mules and twenty men with a large treasure and some furs to trade in Missouri for merchandise to bring back to Mexico. The Chavez family owned much land and many businesses in Mexico, including gold and silver mines. The family was prominent in what is now New Mexico and engaged in much trade between Missouri and New Mexico via the Santa Fe Trail. Chavez's party took the trail's Cimarron Route, which was the shorter route. They ran into bad weather and harsh traveling conditions. One of the two wagons was abandoned, and several mules died. Fifteen men from the Chavez party returned home due to the difficult conditions. Antonio José Chavez continued toward Missouri with a much smaller party.

Captain John McDaniel reportedly had a military commission from the Republic of Texas to raid Mexican merchants on the Santa Fe Trail. Other Texan forces were also planning to raid the trail. Captain McDaniel led a raiding party of fifteen men organized at Yoachum's Tavern in Westport (Kansas City). The Chavez family in New Mexico scheduled annual trading trips from Santa Fe to Missouri via the Santa Fe Trail. McDaniel and his men seem to have known that Chavez was heading up the trail bound for Missouri. This news may have come from a trader or Texas spy in Santa

Fe. McDaniel's group left Westport and headed down the Santa Fe Trail looking for Mexican traders to loot. To those who asked where they were going, McDaniel's men claimed that they were going buffalo hunting. In present-day Rice County, Kansas, at Jarvis Creek (Owl Creek), between April 7 and 10, 1843, Antonio José Chavez's remaining trading party, which was transporting several bales of furs and between $11,000 and $12,000 (1843 value, according to some sources) in gold and silver, was ambushed by McDaniel's party. Chavez and his companions were quickly captured, along with their furs, money and bullion. Most of the gold and silver were in the lone wagon in a wooden chest. The raiders were not well organized, so all of their livestock and Chavez's livestock escaped several days after the Chavez party was captured. They had camped several miles from the Santa Fe Trail on present-day Jarvis Creek to avoid other travelers. Now both the prisoners and their captors were afoot in the wilds of Kansas. The so-called Texas raiders divided up the treasure over several days. As there were fifteen robbers, the splits were not documented as being equal shares or based on priority of command.

Captain John McDaniel wanted to murder Don Antonio José Chavez to prevent him from bringing charges against the McDaniel raiding party. Captain McDaniel knew that his group was no more than outlaws in the guise of being a Texas raiding party. Most of McDaniel's men refused to murder Chavez, as they had come for loot, not murder. Dr. Joseph R. De Prefontaine, John McCormick, Dr. Benjamin T. Harris, Benjamin F. Tolbert, Nathan H. Morton, Christopher Searcy and Gallatin Searcy left McDaniel with their share of the booty and headed for Missouri on foot. As this group approached Council Grove and the Santa Fe Trail, some members were said to have become weary of carrying the heavy money, so they hid their share of the treasure. This group of robbers then separated and entered Missouri to obtain horses to retrieve their hidden treasure.

McDaniel and Joseph Brown shot and murdered Don Antonio José Chavez. From his body, the murderers recovered thirty-nine gold doubloons hidden in his money belt. Fearing they might have missed other treasure, the other robbers searched the wagon again and recovered another $3,000 in gold dust in a trunk. They split the money among themselves. The murderers threw Chavez's body into Jarvis Creek. Chavez's five servants were allowed to leave on foot for Mexico, but without food or weapons. The robbers likely thought the servants would die.

Chavez's servants and others from his party who had escaped spread news of the robbery and the murder of Don Antonio José Chavez. In Westport,

Liberty and other parts of Missouri, posses were organized by traders, merchants and honest men who had been associated with Mexico trading. U.S. Army troops patrolling the Santa Fe Trail from Fort Leavenworth learned of the robbery and the murder of Chavez. These troops also joined the search for McDaniel and his outlaws.

McDaniel threatened to kill Thomas Towson for being unreliable and a threat to the success of the Chavez robbery. Towson fled from Captain McDaniel's group of murderers and robbers without getting a share of the loot. A band of Pottawatomie Indians saved Towson from starvation and death when he was afoot without food.

While John McDaniel's group headed for civilization, they stumbled on some of their horses that had previously escaped their camp. Each man in McDaniel's group thus obtained one horse to ride, with several additional horses to carry the stolen treasure. McDaniel's group then separated, each man carrying his share of the loot.

John McDaniel, David McDaniel and William Mason traveled as a group. On April 24, 1843, at Westport Landing, the McDaniel brothers and Mason sold their horses and bought passage on the steamboat *Weston*. The news about the robbery and murder of Chavez had already arrived in Westport Landing, enraging many in the trading town. A passenger on the *Weston* recognized the three men and alerted authorities in Westport Landing. A posse was formed in the town and rode to intercept the *Weston* at Owens Landing, seeking to apprehend the murderers and robbers.

The McDaniel brothers got off the *Weston* with their loot before the steamer reached Owens Landing. William Mason remained onboard. At Owens Landing, he saw the posse waiting for the vessel on the riverbank. The posse observed Mason throwing an object into the Missouri River before the posse could capture him after the *Weston* arrived. The posse retrieved nine doubloons and a package of papers from the river after Mason was taken prisoner. Part of his share of the loot was not recovered. It might have been thrown into the Missouri River and not recovered, or it might have been hidden elsewhere.

The McDaniel brothers traveled to the town of Liberty, where a posse discovered and arrested them along with gang member Samuel O. Berry. The McDaniels were arrested after they had been in the offices of the Clay County court clerk. The posse confronted the clerk and demanded he either return whatever the McDaniel brothers might have left with him or suffer the consequences of aiding murderers and robbers. The clerk relented and unlocked a secretary drawer that contained $1,500 in coins, which he turned over to the posse. The enraged posse further threatened the clerk with harm if all the loot was not given up to them. After more threats, stolen gold dust and bullion were discovered in a wardrobe in the room. The posse took the loot as evidence.

Joseph Brown had split off from the other members of the McDaniel gang and rode into Camden, Missouri, which is about twenty miles from Liberty, on April 29. Brown sold his horse and boarded the steamboat *Ione*. A posse showed up as the boat departed the landing. The posse got the attention of the *Ione*'s captain and pilot, who returned the steamer to the landing. The posse arrested Joseph Brown on the *Ione* and recovered $500 in silver coins from him.

Even though western Missouri and eastern Kansas had been notified of the robbery and murder, some of the robbers, who now were mounted on horses, decided to recover the loot they had near Council Grove. One of the many posses in the area arrested Dr. De Prefontaine, who had retrieved $2,600 in treasure from his share and the shares of other gang members' caches. When De Prefontaine was captured, he was traveling with tavern owner David Yoachum, who had helped him retrieve the stolen money. The posse also arrested Yoachum, but he was later released because he was not directly involved in the robbery and murder.

Schuyler Oldham escaped capture by the posses and was said to perhaps be heading for Mississippi with his portion of the loot. At Westport Landing, Gallatin Searcy and his brother Christopher, who were part of McDaniel's robbers, later boarded the steamer *Westin*. The Searcy brothers traveled on the *Westin* to Park's Landing, near the town of Parkville, and disappeared from history. Nathaniel H. Morton, William F. Harris and Edward Peyton were captured halfway to Council Grove, Kansas, on the way to recover their share of the hidden treasure. This same posse also captured Thomas Towson.

More than $7,000 in money and bullion were reportedly recovered from the captured robbers At least $3,000 and possibly much more silver and gold were not recovered. Some of the uncovered treasure might have been buried near Council Grove or in western Missouri. Many Missouri traders believed that Chavez's treasure was worth between $30,000 and $32,000, rather than between $11,000 and $12,000, as stated in some accounts. Historically, trading parties from Mexico sometimes carried more than $100,000 in gold and silver to purchase goods in Missouri for transport back to Mexico. Some money thrown into the Missouri River at Owens Landing might still remain.

This international incident between the United States and Mexico halted overland trade to and from Santa Fe and Missouri for a while. Of the fifteen members of Captain McDaniel's raiders, ten were arrested and five escaped capture. John McDaniel and Joseph Brown were tried for murder and robbery and, on August 16, 1845, were executed at St. Louis for Don Chavez's murder. McDaniel and his gang claimed to be Texas soldiers. In spite of their original plans, they did not split the treasure with the Republic of Texas, and they murdered a man in cold blood. The other gang members were tried and convicted. They received fines and prison sentences, except for Berry, who had turned state's evidence and was a free man.

After the trials, the American court returned items to Chavez's family in Mexico: one silver bar weighing about sixty-three pounds, more than four pounds of gold dust, a one-and-a-half-pound gold bar, many silver coins and a medal. This treasure had been recovered and held as evidence by the court and used during the trials. This recovered treasure would be worth more than $130,000 today. How much of the Chavez treasure was hidden and never recovered is unknown. Treasure hunters are known to have looked for the loot in the area of the ambush and Chavez's murder on Jarvis Creek on the Santa Fe Trail.

FATHER DONNELLY'S TREASURE

Father Bernard J. Donnelly was a Catholic priest who started building a brick church in 1857 in Westport Landing, which became Kansas City, Missouri. As Confederate Major General Sterling Price's army marched toward Westport on October 21, 1864, the parishioners of Donnelly's Immaculate Conception Church at Eleventh and Broadway gave their money and valuables to Father Donnelly for safekeeping. The treasure might have been worth between $50,000 and $100,000. Donnelly placed the treasure in a large trunk and buried it in the church cemetery or somewhere on church grounds. A church sexton named Tom helped him cache the treasure. Tom could not keep a secret when he was drunk, and he told people about the cache. Father Donnelly and four others then moved the treasure. It was reported that Donnelly himself moved the treasure to a third location, thought to be north of the church. Some of Donnelly's relatives claimed they saw him bury the treasure and later dig it up.

General Sterling Price's Confederate army was defeated by Union forces at the Battle of Westport on October 23, 1864. This halted the Confederate attempt to capture Westport. The Confederate army headed south. Father Donnelly went to recover the cached funds and treasures of his parishioners, but he could not find it. Donnelly borrowed money from a bank to repay his parishioners for their missing funds. He had a detailed list of everything his parishioners had left in his care.

The land on which the Catholic church and cemetery grounds were located became prime real estate when Kansas City became a major city. Father Donnelly sold forty acres of land in the Quality Hill neighborhood to buy land for a new cemetery, which became Mount St. Mary's Cemetery at Twenty-Second and Cleveland. In 1873, the church started moving graves from the old cemetery to the new one. It is likely that part of the reason for moving the graves was that Father Donnelly was still looking for the lost treasure.

The current Cathedral of Immaculate Conception was started in 1882 and has a gold dome. Father Donnelly died of a heart attack; he never knew what happened to the treasure. The old church is still standing, but the surrounding area has parking lots, apartments and hotels that might be covering the original burial sites. Recent construction found that not all the burials in the old cemetery had been moved.

JESSE JAMES BLUE SPRINGS LOOT

Seven men from the James Gang, including Frank James, robbed the cashier's office at the Kansas City County Fair at Blue Springs on September 26, 1872. The fair, the Kansas City Industrial Exposition, had an attendance of about ten thousand people. The fair receipts had just been tabulated and were awaiting pickup by a special agent of the First National Bank of Kansas City. Three robbers took a chest of money (cashbox) from the fair treasurer. It was said that they stole less than $8,000 ($10,000), but some stories have the robbers taking more than $100,000. Frank Triplett's book claims that only $978 was stolen. A young girl was shot and wounded during the robbery. The gang rode six or seven miles away, then stopped and divided up the loot. They split up and rode in different directions to confuse any subsequent

The notorious robber Jesse James and his gang might have cached loot throughout Missouri. *Library of Congress.*

pose. Some people believe that some of the gang members cached their part of the loot near Blue Springs to lighten the load for their horses so they could travel faster. One tale says that part of the loot was hidden near Dallas, Texas.

MARS

The 329-ton side-wheel steamer *Mars* was built in 1856. It sank at Cogswell Landing on July 8, 1865, about one mile upriver from Napoleon. No lives were lost when the *Mars* sank. A magnetometer investigation by Greg Hawley and his family determined that, with so many oil pipelines in the area, it was too risky to dig for the shipwreck.

JASPER COUNTY

COLE YOUNGER ALBA CACHE

Outlaw Cole Younger of the James-Younger Gang was said to have hidden a large chest of gold and silver coins near Alba.

CONFEDERATE TREASURE

North of Oronogo, just north of Webb City, Confederates supposedly cached a treasure.

KANSAS CITY SOUTHERN ROBBERY LOOT

Between Webb City and Joplin, in 1923, three outlaws reportedly robbed a Kansas City Southern train. They took a heavy strongbox containing money. One robber was captured and claimed the strongbox was buried south of Webb City due to its heavy weight. The other two outlaws were reportedly killed during another robbery. The captured robber later died of illness in prison and thus did not recover the loot.

TOM LIVINGSTON'S CACHE

Miner Thomas "Tom" R. Livingston was said to have come to Missouri from Tennessee. He was heading for the California gold fields but found the lead deposits in Southwest Missouri more to his liking. Another, likely more accurate source claimed that Tom Livingston was born on December 6, 1829, in Montgomery County, Missouri. Tom settled down with his wife, Nancy, west of Carthage. They had three children. Before the Civil War, he was known as "Hawkeye," probably for his ability to discover lead on the ground. Tom and Andrew McKee found a vein of almost pure lead near the surface while digging a cellar in the spring of 1851, and they began mining very rich lead ore. His partner was his half brother William Parkinson. They owned a store, a mine and a lead smelter at French Point, which was two miles west of Minersville. Tom Livingston had a mine and furnace near the Twin Groves community on Center Creek. Livingston had a store, hotel, bar, ranch and much land. According to one story, Livingston employed about one hundred men in his mines and other businesses. He established the mining town of Minersville, which became Oronogo, on Center Creek. A census in 1860 recorded him as being a bachelor. During the Bleeding Kansas border wars, Tom was the captain of a proslavery border guard unit supporting Kansas becoming a slave state. In 1861, there were about twenty-five houses on Center Creek. He also had another mining camp, known as Leadville Hollow. Livingston was a thirty-six-year-old widower with two children when the Civil War began.

Tom Livingston became a Confederate captain and helped raise a regiment of Jasper County men, the Eleventh Cavalry Missouri State Guards. This unit had a short enlistment period and disbanded in February 1862. He later led the First Missouri Battalion (called the Cherokee Spikes or Cherokee Rangers), which was part of the Confederate Provisional Army. The First Missouri Battalion (First Indian Brigade) is said to have included many men from his first regiment, which had disbanded.

Livingston might have led them when they were called Livingston's Rangers. He and his men raided Humboldt and other Kansas towns in retaliation for Union raids on Missouri towns. He reportedly cached $10,000 in gold coins in a metal box during the war near Minersville, not far from Joplin. Livingston had an army camp near French Point and at one time also had a Confederate camp in far southeast Kansas, near the Missouri and Indian Territory borders.

Livingston fought at the Battles of Carthage and Wilson's Creek. On May 13–18, 1863, a Union force marched to the "Centre Creek lead mines,"

Confederate guerrilla Major Tom Livingston owned a lead mine. His treasure is still missing. *State Historical Society of Missouri.*

which were being defended by Tom Livingston and one hundred guerrillas. Livingston and about seventy of his men ambushed a Union foraging party from the First Kansas Colored Infantry Regiment (later the Seventy-Ninth U.S. Colored Infantry Regiment) and the Second Kansas Artillery Battery near Sherwood, Missouri, on May 18, 1863. About twenty-three black Union soldiers and three white Union soldiers were killed in that fight. The black soldiers were probably the first black Union soldiers killed in the Civil War. Three white soldiers and two black soldiers were captured by Livingston's troops. Union troops destroyed the buildings in French Point. In *The War of the Rebellion: A Compilation of the Official Records of the Union and Confederate Armies*, Major T.R. Livingston wrote a report from Diamond Grove in Jasper County detailing his actions from May 16 to 19. He was slightly wounded during the battle at Sherwood. He wrote that captured white Union prisoners were quickly exchanged for Confederate prisoners and that the Union forces burned the town of Sherwood and eleven nearby farms. The residents of Sherwood reportedly fled to Texas as refugees, and the town was never rebuilt.

One of the black soldiers was murdered by someone not under his command, according to Livingston. Colonel James Monroe Williams of the

First Kansas Colored Infantry Regiment commanded that the man who murdered the Union soldier be turned over to him. Livingston refused or did not have the murderer under his control. Colonel Williams hanged a captured Confederate soldier. Livingston then had a captured black Union soldier hanged in retaliation. Williams and Livingston thereafter often murdered captured soldiers. There had been confusion among the Union troops during the battle, as many of the Confederates wore blue uniforms likely taken from Union soldiers.

Major Tom Livingston was killed when he led one hundred Confederate irregulars in an attack against the Cedar County Courthouse in Stockton on July 11, 1863. There were twenty Union soldiers of the Twenty-Sixth Regiment Missouri Militia defending the courthouse. Livingston wore body armor under his shirt and was shot off his horse. Several Union soldiers shot him when he tried to get up. He was also reportedly clubbed to death with a pistol by one of the Union soldiers.

According to one story, his wife and son looked for a buffalo-shaped rock, which was a marker to Livingston's treasure. W.C. Jameson's *Lost Mines and Buried Treasures of Missouri* tells of a hiker in the 1970s who was exploring and taking pictures in the ghost town of Minersville. One of his photos included a buffalo-shaped rock about three feet high. The hiker's friend in Joplin saw the photo and commented on Livingston's lost cache. They returned to Minersville but did not report finding the buffalo-shaped rock or Livingston's treasure.

JEFFERSON COUNTY

BIG RIVER CACHE

See Washington County.

LOST SILVER MINE

In the Rockfort area south of Herculaneum, a Frenchman reportedly mined silver ore, which he then smuggled to New Orleans to avoid taxes.

Johnson County

Migrant Train Cache

In the summer of 1825, a wagon train of migrants reportedly heading west stopped in Georgetown for a few days before heading out through Indian lands. It was thought they then traveled three days west to Big Walnut Creek and camped on the north side of Twin Knobs. They were known by the people in Georgetown to have gold and silver coins and a treasurer who hid the money every time they camped for the night. In 1829, the remains of burned-out wagons and debris were recorded on the north side of Twin Knobs. It was thought that an Indian tribe, perhaps the Osage, might have attacked the camped wagon train and killed everyone before burning the wagons. The money may have been cached and might still be in this area.

Laclede County

California Miner's Gold

A miner returning from the California gold fields was said to have cached $60,000 in gold at a Gasconade River ford about seven miles west of Lynchburg and twenty-five miles west of Rolla. The miner was killed by outlaws, and his cache was lost.

Guerrilla leader William C. Quantrill supposedly buried a fortune above the Meramec River. *Library of Congress*.

Quantrill's Treasure

Confederate guerrilla leader William C. Quantrill reportedly buried about $10 million in a cliff above the Meramec River near Belle Starr's Needle in the present-day national forest. It is unlikely that Quantrill ever had such a large sum of money, but he might have hidden something.

Lafayette County

Mars

See Jackson County.

Princess

The 185-ton *Princess* was built in 1863. It was stranded on July 1, 1868, near Napoleon with supplies bound for Fort Benton in Montana. No lives were lost when it wrecked.

Saluda

The 223-ton steamboat *Saluda* was built in 1846. It exploded on April 9, 1852, above Lexington on the Missouri River with a death toll of thirty-five (twenty-seven). Another source claimed that more than one hundred bodies were removed from the wreck and river. Captain Bell and pilot Charles La Barge were killed. The boat was carrying Mormon migrants bound for Council Bluffs who planned to travel the Mormon Trail to Utah. The surviving children of the dead Mormons were adopted by citizens in Lexington, and some of them became noted citizens of the town. The *Saluda* had previously been snagged and sank five miles below Rocheport. Its hull was dug out of the bar that formed around this first wreck. It had been rebuilt in St. Louis.

Stage Station Treasure

In 1861 or 1862, John C. Underwood and another man stayed at a stage station or inn along the Lexington-Warrensburg Road. The two men reportedly had a large sum of gold coins, which they cached near the stage station. Later, Underwood killed his companion in a fight in the stage station yard and fled from the area.

Underwood joined the Confederate army in Arkansas. He was said to have told a fellow soldier named Brent about the hidden gold coins. Underwood also showed Brent a map of his cache when Underwood was in an army field hospital at Fort Smith, Arkansas, after he was wounded. Underwood died from his wounds, so Brent acquired the treasure map.

When the Civil War ended, Brent returned to his home in southeastern Missouri and never searched for the gold cache. He told his nephew Jerry Montgomery about the treasure. Montgomery knew a man in Advance, Missouri, T.E. Austin, who had once lived in Lafayette County. In 1896, Montgomery wrote to Austin about the treasure. Austin wrote to a friend, a Mr. Powell, and sent the map to him. Powell searched for treasure at what he thought was the old stage station but reportedly found no treasure. The gold coins could still be hidden.

WILLIAM BAIRD

The 286-ton steamship William Baird was built in 1855. It sank on a snag in 1858 opposite Waverly, Missouri, while carrying about 150 passengers, whiskey and $5,000 in gold. No lives were lost when it sank. It was found using a magnetometer and drilling by Greg Hawley and his family and investors. The William Baird's stern was under a U.S. Army Corps of Engineers levee, which would have had to be moved and rebuilt in order to access the ship. It was estimated to cost about $100,000 to do so, so the project was abandoned by Hawley and his group.

LAWRENCE COUNTY

FARRINGTON TREASURE

The Mobile & Ohio Flyer Railroad train was robbed of more than $70,000 at Union City, Tennessee, in 1870 by brothers Levi and Hillary Farrington and two other outlaws. The Farrington brothers were said to have ridden with William Quantrill during the Civil War. Pinkerton agents trapped and captured Hillary at an old farmhouse near Verona, Missouri. While being transported on a riverboat heading to Union City, Tennessee, for trial, Hillary got into a fight with his guards. He was knocked overboard into the steamer's paddle wheel and killed. Levi Farrington was soon captured by lawmen and taken to Union City for trial. A mob there took Levi from the jail and lynched him before he could be tried. Pinkerton detectives searched the Verona farmhouse and surrounding area but were unable to find what they thought was $8,000 taken by Hillary from two different robberies. This may be the same story as that listed under "Hillary Farrington Treasure" in Stone County.

TURKEY TRACKS SPANISH TREASURE

A legend published in the *Ozark Mountaineer* claimed that early settlers in the area found large turkey tracks carved into a limestone ledge heading south toward a spring. The ledge was near Mill Creek and Turnback Creek on the Cliff Morris farm. Supposedly, the turkey tracks pointed to a buried Spanish treasure. A man with a map was said to have come to the area over several years looking for this treasure. Hutton Adamson of Miller was the source of this *Ozark Mountaineer* tale. It was a popular story discussed for many years by residents of the area.

LEWIS AND CLARK COUNTY

AUGUSTA TREASURE

Near Augusta, some $60,000 in gold coins were said to have been cached.

LINN COUNTY

TREASURE CAVE

A treasure cave in Linn County is associated with some sort of lost treasure.

MARION COUNTY

MARK TWAIN CAVE TREASURES

Just a few miles south of Hannibal, along the Mississippi River, is what is popularly known today as Mark Twain Cave. This cave was previously called McDowell's Cave, Sim's Cave and Big Salt-peter Cave. It was made famous by Mark Twain's *The Adventures of Tom Sawyer* as the site where Injun Joe hid

Left: Mark Twain's *The Adventures of Tom Sawyer* made the Mark Twain Cave famous as the site of Injun Joe's treasure. *Library of Congress.*

Below: The Mark Twain Cave entrance in the 1930s. Legends claim that several treasures were cached there. *Historical Society of Missouri.*

his treasure, which Tom Sawyer and Becky Thatcher find. Mark Twain was Samuel Clemens's pen name. Clemens moved to Hannibal in 1839 from Florida, Missouri, with his family. He grew up in Hannibal and was familiar with the cave, which he visited often as a child and young man. Clemens wrote many books about Missouri and the Mississippi River.

There is a legend that '49er California prospectors hid gold in Mark Twain Cave. The cave is actually a complex of fissures in limestone that have interconnecting tunnels and cracks over a large area. During the Civil War, Confederates stored weapons in the cave. Jesse James and his gang were said to have used the cave as a hideout.

Gold ingots salvaged from a Civil War steamboat were supposedly hidden between the Mississippi River and Mark Twain Cave. A number of steamboats sank in this area during the war, so there could be some basis for this tale.

McDonald County

Ford Meadows Treasure

About $75,000 in gold and silver coins were rumored to have been cached near Bethpage in Ford Meadows.

Found Fort Crowder Treasure

See Newton County.

Lost Sugar River Gold Mine

In the late 1700s and early 1800s, Spaniards reportedly mined gold on the Big Sugar River near present-day Pineville. The Spaniards were attacked, and most of them were killed. The surviving Spaniards supposedly hid the gold ore and gold bullion before fleeing the area. The mine with its gold cache was supposed to be near the Missouri-Arkansas border southeast of Pineville.

Madre Vena Cave Treasure

Spanish miners reportedly stored one year's worth of their mined gold bullion in the Madre Vena Cave (Mother Vein Cave) in the Madre Vena Mountains sometime in the mid-1700s. Madre Vena Cave is in Pea Ridge Hollow, which was about half a mile from the old Bear Hollow School. One story has this mine located between Bentonville, Arkansas, and Jane, Missouri. In 1802, an epidemic was said to have killed most of the Spanish miners. The survivors hid the cave entrance and went to Mexico. Some returned after a couple of years away, but a forest fire had removed most of their landmarks, and they couldn't find the cave with their gold. In 1860, an old man who was a descendant of the miners visited Pierce City, looking for the cave and treasure. When he was dying, the man told the doctor who treated him about the cave and treasure and gave him directions. This tale may be a variation of the "Spanish Miners Bear Hollow Gold" tale that follows.

OZARK WONDER CAVE AREA MINE

The Ozark Wonder Cave, 420 feet long, was developed as a tourist cave in 1915 by J.A. Truitt. He developed other show caves in the area. This was the first show cave in McDonald County. The Spanish reportedly had mines in the area near Noel and Jane. During the Civil War, legends claimed that several wagons of gold were dumped into a shaft nearby. Confederate Missouri Governor Claiborne Fox Jackson was said to have held a meeting of the successionist Missouri legislature in the Ozark Wonder Cave.

SPANISH MINERS BEAR HOLLOW GOLD

A party of Spanish miners traveling to New Orleans after a successful mining trip in the West was reportedly attacked by Indians near Bear Hollow (Bear Tree Hollow). The Indians killed several miners and wounded others in the party. The pack animals were killed or scattered. The Spanish miners reportedly had thirty bags of gold and silver with them, which they hid in a rock crevice. Some articles on this treasure claim the cache was worth more than $1 million. Water was then diverted by the miners to hide the gold cache. This gold might have been hidden in a cave. This cave was called Bear Hollow Cave, but other people claimed it was the Linderman Cave. It was said to be south of Pineville and north of Bentonville, Arkansas, and east of Caverna. Caverna sits on the state line of McDonald County in Missouri and Benton County in Arkansas. The surviving Spanish miners fled to Mexico or possibly to Pensacola in present-day Florida. Florida was a Spanish colony at that time.

Several sources of this lost treasure exist. Bob Walker heard of the treasure from a dying Mexican who was in a Confederate army prison camp during the Civil War. An old Mexican woman visited Guy Van Werner's farm in what is now Oklahoma. For his kindness to her, she gave Van Werner (Van Warmer, Vanworner) her father's map of the treasure cache from the 1700s. In 1884, Van Werner carried the map of the buried gold and searched for it near the town of Lanagan in Southwest Missouri. Van Werner and John Koch of Afton, Oklahoma, looked for the treasure together. They found a cave with an inner chamber full of water that they were unable to drain using pumps. In 1928 or 1927, Guy Van Werner's son looked for it and found three graves that were thought to have been part of the original Spanish mining party.

Frank Fiant, Becheld Smith and Enoch Hodson also searched for the treasure. In 1929, Charley Nidiffin looked for the gold without finding it. In 1932, Charles Bootman, a geophysicist and prospector, came to the area and reportedly spent $100,000 looking for the treasure. While some thought it was in the cave, others believed it was hidden outside the cave. In the 1930s, Herb Lipps of Enid, Oklahoma, leased about one thousand acres in the area to look for gold and silver. Some gold-bearing sand was reportedly found. It was assayed at $2 to $8,000 per ton (two thousand pounds).

In 1955, Beeler Porterfield saw steam rising from the ground on a cold day and figured there was a cave entrance below. He dug down four feet and found a blocked cave entrance. Using a sledgehammer, he broke through the rock covering the entrance. He went inside what turned out to be a seventy-foot-long cave. The rest of the cave was filled with rock and soil debris.

Some think the original cave entrance was on land of the resort of Bella Vista Village. Some versions of this story claim the treasure was near Pineview. This is a variation of the Madre Vena Cave treasure story. Some variations of these tales have locations in Arkansas, such as the Hurricane Creek Silver Mine near Devil's Den State Park in the Boston Mountains.

Other versions of this story claim the lost Spanish treasure was near Sulphur Springs, Arkansas. In Arkansas, a similar story was associated with Old Spanish Cave about three miles south of Sulphur Springs. See also "Madre Vena Cave Treasure" in McDonald County.

SPLITLOG MINE AND CACHE

Mathias Splitlog was a Cayuga Indian born in New York or possibly in Canada. He was half French Canadian and half Cayuga by blood. He married a Wyandotte woman in Ohio and migrated with the Wyandotte tribe to Kansas Territory in 1843. He was a wise businessman who grew rich with his various endeavors. He was involved in mining, milling, manufacturing and real estate.

In 1887, Splitlog and his investors lost money in a gold and silver mining investment that turned out to have no gold or silver in the mine in McDonald County. The Spitlog Land and Mining Company leased about five thousand acres to develop gold mines. The promoter, M.C. Clay, reportedly got some gold ore from a real Colorado gold mine and claimed it was from a Missouri mine he was raising money to develop. Splitlog supplied him money but never saw any profit from this venture. A railroad was planned to this mine and other mines to be developed in the area. The railroad tracks were only partially laid before Clay's scheme collapsed and he fled from the area. The railroad company, the Kansas City, Fort Smith and Southern Railway Company, was reportedly capitalized for $3 million. This railroad later became part of the Kansas City Southern Railway.

Mathias Splitlog established the town of Splitlog in McDonald County and Cayuga Springs in Indian Territory on the Wyandotte Indian Reservation. The town of Splitlog was near Splitlog's mine, about four miles northwest of the present-day town of Anderson. Splitlog died on January 2, 1893, when he reached Washington, D.C., to represent the Wyandotte Indians. He was thought by some to have hidden a cache of money in Missouri, as he normally did business with gold coins rather than currency or checks. It seems unlikely that such a cache would be in Missouri, as he spent his remaining days in present-day Oklahoma. There is a legend, however, that Splitlog hid money in Missouri.

MILLER COUNTY

RAMSEY CAVE TREASURE

A legend claimed that seven loads of gold were buried in Ramsey Cave during the Civil War. The cave is on a wooded ridge. A rope and ladder are required to get down thirty feet to its entrance. The cave is three hundred feet long. In 1929, treasure hunters used blasting powder in their search for the cache in and near Ramsey Cave.

MISSISSIPPI COUNTY

CHARLESTON TREASURE

A Charleston bank was robbed of $100,000 during the Civil War, and the money was said to have been buried outside of Charleston. The robbers were then killed before they could dig up the loot. A bank cashier hid $55,000 in a trash barrel during the robbery, which the robbers missed.

This story may be based on the deeds of the "Missouri Swamp Fox," Confederate Colonel Meriweather Jeff "M. Jeff" Thompson, who led a group of his Confederate soldiers to rob a bank in August 1861 in Charleston,

Left: The "Missouri Swamp Fox," M. Jeff Thompson, and his men robbed a Charleston bank. What happened to the loot is unknown. *Library of Congress*.

Below: The Union army camp at Cape Girardeau probably persuaded M. Jeff Thompson from robbing a local bank there. *Missouri Historical Society*.

Missouri, of $55,000 ($56,000) in order to finance his forces. Thompson's Confederate troops disappeared into Mingo Swamp in Stoddard County, which is now part of Mingo National Wildlife Refuge. There were different versions of what happened to the stolen bank funds. One version was that the funds were used to supply and arm Confederate soldiers under Thompson's command. Another story was that all or most of the funds were returned to the bank depositors, most of whom were Confederates. Thompson originally was going to rob a bank in Cape Girardeau but reportedly changed his mind and robbed the bank in Charleston. The presence of Union troops in Cape Girardeau likely was a factor in his decision. He had a long political and military career. Thompson became a Confederate brigadier general who led troops in many battles.

TREASURE OF THE STEAMER *RUTH*

The 702-ton side-wheel steamboat *Ruth* was built in February 1863 at a cost of $70,000. Due to the Civil War and the growing need for vessels, its value appreciated to $100,000. Caroline Peyram, Captain Peyram's mother, actually owned the *Ruth*, which had been specifically constructed to transport people and cargo on the Mississippi River.

On July 29, 1863, the U.S. Treasury at Washington, D.C., transferred $3 million in U.S. currency to Adams Express Company for shipment to St. Louis. When the money arrived, the U.S. Army funds were turned over to Assistant U.S. Treasurer Benjamin Farrar. The money was put into a wagon driven by a Mr. Goddard on August 3. Union treasury agents delivered $2.6 million in greenbacks packed in four boxes to army paymaster Major Nathan S. Brinton. Box No. 1 held $120,000 in $1 notes; Box No. 2 contained $120,000 in $2 notes and $300,000 in $5 notes; and Box No. 4 contained $800,000 of $10 notes and $800,000 of $20 notes. In St. Louis, Box No. 3 was opened, and $240,000 from this shipment was removed and put into the care of Assistant Treasurer Farrar. The remaining $460,000 in $5 and $10 notes from this box were transferred to Major Nathan S. Brinton.

Major Brinton took the cash by wagon through the St. Louis business district to the steamer *Ruth*, which was docked on the Mississippi River landing. A guard of thirty-one soldiers of Company I, Ninth Wisconsin, along with eight paymasters and their clerks, were assigned to the *Ruth* to protect the huge payroll. On the vessel, the money was secured in the eight paymasters' iron safes and in eight boxes on the cabin deck.

Major General Ulysses S. Grant's army's $2.6 million payroll was aboard the steamboat *Ruth*, which Confederate agents burned. *Library of Congress.*

On August 3, the *Ruth* departed St. Louis carrying about 150 people, including Union soldiers. The ship's itinerary was Cairo, Illinois; Memphis, Tennessee; Helena, Arkansas; and Vicksburg, Mississippi, on the way with the $2.6 million in cash to pay Major General Ulysses S. Grant's Union army. Vicksburg had surrendered to Grant's army on July 4, 1863. The victorious Union forces now controlled the Mississippi River and needed to be paid.

On August 4 at 7:00 p.m., the *Ruth* arrived at Cairo on the Ohio River and docked for two hours before heading downstream to the Mississippi River. The previous night at the U.S. Naval Depot in Cairo, a suspicious fire was discovered. This blaze was likely set by Confederate agents. The *Ruth*, as it departed Cairo, carried 99 cattle, 122 mules, 400 tons of commissary and sutler's stores, 100 tons of private freight, several passengers and the $2.6 million army payroll in cash.

At about midnight about eight miles below Cairo, opposite Island No. 1, the *Ruth* was discovered to be on fire between its aft decks. It was later believed that Confederate agents set the fire in the carpenter's shop. The steamer's crew immediately fled from their stations. Although one of the steamer's paddle wheels had stopped, the other paddle wheel continued rotating at full speed. The *Ruth* swung around and steamed into a thirty-foot-high Missouri bank at full force. A wooden plank was run from the *Ruth* to the shore as people rushed off the burning steamer for the safety of the riverbank. A chain from the *Ruth* was tied to the bank in an effort to secure the steamer to shore. Most of the passengers and crew either went ashore on the plank or jumped overboard to swim to shore. A stage plank fell on the boat, killing three Union soldiers.

With one paddle wheel still turning, the *Ruth* swung from shore and headed downstream with at least twenty people on board, including some guards. The Union soldiers guarding the payroll were reluctant to leave their posts. In about five minutes, the fire engulfed the *Ruth*. The burning steamboat lit up the dark night and alerted all in the area that a steamboat was in distress.

After twenty minutes of the blaze, the paymasters' safes and payroll boxes fell ten feet through the burned-out cabin deck onto burning coal and a cargo of bacon. The *Ruth* burned until 6:00 a.m. on August 5, when its hull finally gave way and the vessel sank in eighteen feet of water, stern foremost, at Lucas Bend, about four miles below the village of Norfolk, Missouri. Norfolk is now another long-gone river community done in by flooding and erosion. People from the Illinois and Missouri sides of the Mississippi River arrived in small boats to rescue survivors and recover valuables from the wreck. It appeared to everyone present that the fire had consumed everything on the *Ruth*. The steamer *Spanish* finally came to the wreck site and picked up the survivors on the riverbank. The survivors were taken back to Cairo.

Among the twenty-six (thirty) people killed or missing in the tragedy were two African American deckhands, a chambermaid, an African American woman, one Union corporal, four Union privates and three Union paymaster clerks. The *Ruth*'s captain and most of the crew survived the wreck. The ship's books were taken ashore when the fire started. To prevent anyone from recovering the $2.6 million payroll, the Union army posted a guard at the wreck site.

Secretary of the Treasury Salmon P. Chase designated treasury agent H.G. Root on August 31, 1863, to control operations to salvage the sunken Union payroll on the *Ruth* and to investigate the cause of its fire and sinking. The U.S. Army paid salvage divers to search the wreck and recover what they could, especially the Union payroll. Diver Felix Jourand had twenty years of experience diving on and salvaging shipwrecks. Jourand examined the wreck from his submarine armor from August 29 to October 18. Jourand and his divers recovered scattered fragments of charred treasury notes and four of the eight paymaster's chests, which contained nothing but charred currency. The treasury notes had mostly disintegrated, but pieces of one-dollar, two-dollar and twenty-dollar notes were retrieved from Boxes No. 2 and No. 4. Debris clogged the inside of the sunken *Ruth*. The Union War Department's contract divers also recovered iron, machinery and some cargo. The steamer's bell had been fused by the heat. Three of the *Ruth*'s boilers had been burned and warped into unusable shapes. The divers reported that the *Ruth* had been completely gutted by fire before sinking. On October 19, to prevent any nongovernment salvage attempts, the remains of the *Ruth* were blown up with gunpowder. It appears that four paymaster's chests may still be on the shipwreck or nearby.

To investigate and determine facts on the loss of the Union payroll, a court of inquiry was held at St. Louis on September 21, 1863, with Union Major General David Hunter heading the court. The court of inquiry decided that Confederate agents probably set the fire using an incendiary. They ruled that no government officer or agent of the funds was to blame for misconduct or neglect of duty in the sinking of the steamer *Ruth* and the loss of so much Union currency.

Under normal government and army rules, Major Nathan S. Brinton and all the army paymasters who signed for the payroll in St. Louis were personally liable for the loss of the funds on the *Ruth*. Despite the U.S. Army and the U.S. Treasury Department both clearing the paymasters of any wrongdoing, the men could be excused from liability for the loss of the payroll only by acts of the U.S. Congress. From July to December 1864, in order to clear each paymaster of personal liability, bills were enacted. These private bills were passed by both the House of Representatives and the Senate. President Abraham Lincoln then signed each bill, and the paymasters were removed from liability and their accounts settled.

It is possible that some of the *Ruth*'s payroll of U.S. currency remains buried in the Mississippi mud. Paper from Civil War shipwrecks the *Bertrand* in Nebraska and the USS *Cairo* in Mississippi were salvaged in recent times. Paper material was still readable after recovery. It would be hard to locate the remains of the *Ruth*, since its boilers and machinery were removed during salvage in 1863. A magnetometer would likely not receive a big signal above the wreck. Undoubtedly, much navigation work by the U.S. Army Corps of Engineers and others could have been done at the wreck site. Changes in the river channel may have put the wreck under mostly dry land, but it could still be underwater.

MONITEAU COUNTY

BRUCE CAVE CACHE

Bruce Cave is a 1,055-foot-long cave. Blackbeard the river pirate supposedly was being chased by a posse when he hid his loot in or near Bruce Cave. A doodlebugger was convinced there was treasure in the cave, so it was drilled and dynamited, but no treasure was found. According to one legend, forty pack mules worth of gold were hidden nearby. There is also a different Bruce Cave in Pulaski County and Ste. Genevieve County.

MONTGOMERY COUNTY

FOUND TREASURE CHEST

See Butler County.

LOST LOUISIANA MINE

The remains of an old mine are located about one mile southwest of Bear City near the Golden Wonder Cave. This mine was developed with a 460-foot-deep shaft, and it supposedly yielded gold and silver. Some believe this was the "Lost Louisiana Mine," which others believe was in Arkansas, not in Missouri.

NEWTON COUNTY

FOUND FORT CROWDER TREASURE

At Fort Crowder, soldiers reportedly discovered several caches of 1800s gold and silver. Camp Crowder was built during World War II and covered sixty-one thousand acres in McDonald and Newton Counties.

HICKMAN TREASURE

Ray (or John) Hickman was a wealthy rancher who lived just southwest of Joplin on Shoal Creek. Hickman may have buried his money on or near his ranch. He ran cattle in Missouri, Indian Territory and Kansas. Hickman was reportedly tortured by several bushwhackers who wanted his money. In 1862, a Union foraging party found Hickman murdered at his ranch. His murderers may have been soldiers looking for his treasure. Some believe Hickman's treasure was not recovered by his murderers.

SPANISH JEWELRY

In 1745, a band of Spaniards came to the New World in search of treasure. It is said that during this journey they carried an iron pot with valuable jewelry. Only one member of the expedition survived and made it back to Spain. There, he refused to talk about what happened to his companions in the New World. The Spaniard secluded himself in his family's ancestral home and later died.

About 1870, the grandson of the Spanish survivor discovered his grandfather's snuffbox while remodeling the family's home. Inside was yellowed paper detailing the Spanish party's search for wealth in the New World. The group of Spaniards had traveled up the Mississippi River to the Arkansas River and then to what is thought to be Dardanelle, Arkansas. From Dardanelle, which is located about one hundred miles up the Arkansas River, they traveled fifteen days' north. They buried the jewelry box in a spot halfway between a waterfall and a creek due north. A key marker to the treasure was a large, flat rock with an arrow carved on it. The jewelry was buried ten steps east and ten steps south of this marked rock.

Near Neosho, Missouri, the grandson searched for the jewelry box in 1880. Near a falls, with the first creek north being Turkey Creek, he reportedly found the marked rock, but no treasure. See "Turkey Creek Spanish Treasure."

TURKEY CREEK SPANISH TREASURE

Two men dowsing for Spanish treasure about 1849 instead found mostly lead on Turkey Creek. This find later became a major lead and zinc mining area in the Tri-State Mining District. But it is said that the men found an old pouch with some Spanish coins and jewels during their exploration in the area. This story might be related to the previous story, "Spanish Jewelry." One of the men left to find gold in California; the other stayed behind and mined lead and zinc.

NODAWAY COUNTY

LYNN TALBOT'S TREASURE

The House of the Seven Gables is a few (eight) miles north of Barnard on U.S. Highway 71 North. The house was owned by Dr. Lynn Talbot (Talbott). Dr. Talbot was rumored to have buried a nail keg full of $5, $10 and $20 gold pieces close to his home. Talbot's treasure was said to be worth more than $500,000 in today's terms. Dr. Talbot was murdered on November or December 12, 1879, and his treasure was lost. According to the tale, a window was opened slightly, and Dr. Talbot's wife was in their kitchen when she heard a shot fired. On coming into the room, his wife found her husband dead in his chair. He had been shot in the head. It turned out that his sons, Charles E. and Albert P. Talbot, killed their father to get his hidden gold. The brothers searched for the gold but never found it.

A detective by the name of Chandler gained the confidence of the two brothers and worked undercover as a farmhand. He gathered information that implicated the brothers for the murder. The Talbot brothers were tried in 1881 for murder, and both men were convicted. They were executed soon after the trial. To murder their father, it was thought that one son held up the window curtain while the other son, standing outside, fired his gun through the window opening.

OSAGE COUNTY

MOLLIE DOZZIER

See Callaway County.

OZARK COUNTY

JESSE JAMES CACHE

The outlaw Jesse James and his gang reportedly stashed $100,000 in a cave near Gainesville.

SPANISH PERUVIAN TREASURE AND LOST MINE

See Douglas County.

PHELPS COUNTY

GOURD CREEK CAVE

This cave has a long history of human habitation. It is 550 feet long and was used as a refuge during the Civil War. A treasure legend has been associated with this cave.

POLK COUNTY

LOST MISSOURI MINE

See Dallas County.

NOBLE HILL SPANISH MINE

According to legend, on Noble Hill near the Polk County–Greene County line, about thirteen miles north of Springfield, was an old Spanish mine. Between 1940 and 1946, a Mr. Mullen had his eighty acres surveyed on the top of Noble Hill. When the land was surveyed, two old guns and piles of stones (including flat stones with marks cut into them) were found. Mullen's son Bill was ten years old at the time. Bill Mullen's son later remembered wondering about the many piled-up rocks that people thought were from an old mine. This likely was an old lead and zinc mine or prospect. Some people thought a treasure was located nearby.

PULASKI COUNTY

FOUND SILVER DOLLARS

At the Capehart housing project near Fort Leonard Wood Military Reservation, a bulldozer unearthed two big boxes close to the Roubidoux River. The boxes contained about four thousand silver dollars from the late 1880s.

LIMONITE GOLD

A sample of limonite in small outcrops in NE Section 5, T1S, R17W reportedly had traces of gold and silver from June 1887 samples that were tested. Blocher Road goes through the valley, and the samples were said to have been taken near the top of a low ridge near a sulfur spring.

LOST POSSUM LODGE TREASURE

The fishing camp called Possum Lodge on either the Big Piney River or Gasconade River had a ford used by travelers. Outlaw Jesse James and his gang camped at or near Possum Lodge and reportedly hid loot in the nearby hills. This camp was east of Waynesville near the Phelps County line. One legend claimed a miner returning east from the California gold fields became ill, so he buried $60,000 in gold near Possum Lodge and then died.

TILLEY FARM CACHE

When the Civil War started, Wilson M. Tilley was a successful farmer and rich businessman living near Waynesville. Not trusting banks, he reportedly hid his fortune in coins in four chests on or near his farm. Being a Confederate sympathizer, he knew his fortune was at risk. One day, a group of bushwhackers or Union soldiers came to his farm after hearing he had hidden his money nearby. They ordered him to turn over his money. He refused. They beat him, and he still refused. Finally, they put a noose around his neck and threatened to hang him. Tilley refused. In frustration, they hanged him and looted his farm. His body was found a few days later.

In 1962, at or near the old Tilley farm, about four miles south of Waynesville near Route 4, a bulldozer was clearing farmland. As it plowed across a field, the bulldozer operator noticed several objects being uncovered in the field as a result of his plowing. On examination, he found two wooden chests containing coins that ranged from dimes to dollars and dated between 1841 and 1862. Since there was a story that Tilley had buried four chests, people began to search the field. No one reported finding the rest of William Tilley's life savings.

Putnam County

Ed Henson Treasure

Ed Henson had a farm near Unionville and died in 1949. Henson also had a sawmill and a freight company. He was known to have a lot of silver coins. After his death, the purchaser of Henson's farm found a handwritten will in an old can. The 1942 will claimed that Henson had buried almost $40,000 in silver coins inside jars and cans. The will let his children know he had buried a fruit jar containing money on his land. His family found a fruit jar with $4,600. Another version of this story says that in 1964 a farmer plowing a field on the old Henson farm uncovered a coffee can full of silver dollars

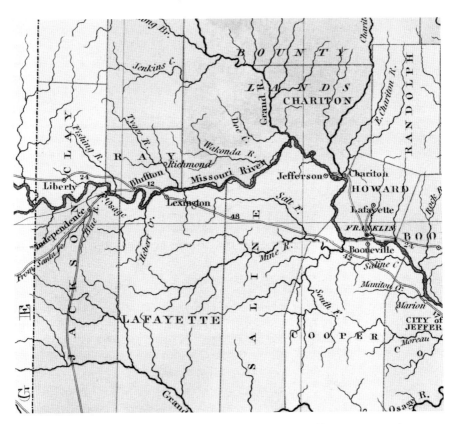

This 1833 map covers an area with many sunken steamboats and lost treasure on the Missouri River. *Missouri Historical Society.*

near the fence line on the west side of the field. There was a belief that Ed Henson had hidden more cash after he wrote his will. It was thought that more of his buried silver was likely still hidden on Henson's farm.

Rallis County

Mark Twain Cave Treasures

See Marion County.

Ray County

Mars

See Jackson County.

Princess

See Lafayette County.

Reynold County

Black River Silver Mine

Indians and Spaniards supposedly mined silver near the Black River. They carried the ore in buckskin bags to the Current River, smelted it and then used canoes to transport it downstream to New Orleans to trade for supplies.

Shannon County

Slater's Lost Mine Found

Joseph Slater found a rich copper deposit near the junction of the Current and Jacks Fork Rivers about 1830. Slater lived in the area until the 1850s.

A 1920s article in a Kansas City newspaper claimed that he sold $50,000 in copper ore over several years by floating it down the Current, Black, White and Mississippi Rivers to New Orleans. Slater didn't actually own the land, so he hid his mine and eventually abandoned it. Slater's Mine was said to have been lost. During the Great Depression, several groups of prospectors reportedly searched for this lost mine. Several treasure magazines and books included stories about this lost mine. I became interested in this story, as I was familiar with the area. In 1986, *Treasure Search* magazine published my article on my search for this supposedly lost mine.

The June 20, 1840 edition of *Niles Register* announced that copper had been found in Missouri in the Current River area. I located an 1877 book by the Missouri state geologist, Dr. Charles P. Williams, titled *Industrial Report on Lead, Zinc, and Iron, Together with Notes on Shannon County and Its Copper Deposits*. Dr. Williams's work said that Slater had started mining in 1830 in the NW NE Section 36, T29N, R4W, which was only one mile southeast of Eminence. This legal description of the mine covers about forty acres. The copper deposits were located at the boundary contact of the Precambrian-age rhyolite (a granite) and tuff (a granite) and the Cambrian-age Eminence dolostone. The copper was found in a limestone-dolostone quartz porphyry. Slater mined about 1,500 tons of ore, which was smelted on the site with some ore shipped to Swanson, Missouri. The ore was said to be 22 percent metallic copper, which was very rich ore. A lawsuit stopped Slater from mining further, probably because he did not actually own the land on which the mine was located. Another source noted that in the Eminence area between 1838 and 1840, 300 short tons of copper had been produced worth $120,000 at the time. The Aberdeen (Scotland) Mining Company reopened Slater's Mine. The Current Mining Company was also involved in the site of the mine. About 1875, the Consolidated Mining Company operated Slater's Mine and also reprocessed the spoils using better technology to recover more copper. Mining in the Eminence area was active into the late 1920s. Slater's Spring is located nearby and can be found on maps.

SINKING CREEK SILVER MINE

An old silver mine was said to have been located near Sinking Creek. Green Carroll reportedly found the mine in 1873. Green worked the silver mine for years with his partner. In 1881, Green and his partner were found shot. Carroll's partner was dead; Carroll later died. Before he died, Green Carroll told his doctor, Dr. Abijah Terrel (Tyrell), about the lost mine and his hidden life's savings. Carroll had hidden his money one mile east of twin springs in a gulch east of a tree with a broken limb, thirty feet above the ground. Dr. Terrel bought the land he believed was in the area of the lost mine. He and his son hunted for the silver mine and treasure cache. He built a house but never found a lost mine there. Some think the mine was near the Current River. A cave called Carroll's Cave is in the area and is about one mile long.

St. Charles County

Bedford

On April 25, 1854, during a fierce storm, the side-wheel, single-engine steamboat *Bedford* hit a snag, tearing a big hole in its hull. The ship began to immediately fill with water and sank in about one minute to its hurricane deck. Twelve to fourteen people died in the sinking. One passenger lost his trunk containing $6,000 in specie. The boat was valued at $10,000 at the time but was insured for only $3,000. The boat and its cargo were reported as a total loss.

The city of St. Charles had a number of Missouri River steamboat shipwrecks nearby. *Missouri Historical Society*.

EDNA

The side-wheel Glasgow packet *Edna* was carrying German immigrants when its boiler exploded near Green Island at the mouth of the Missouri River on July 2, 1842 (June 14, 1847). The explosion caused the flues to collapse. Fifty-five (forty-five) German immigrants were killed. This could be in St. Louis County.

FOUND CACHES

Several small caches of gold coins were reportedly found about one mile northwest of the Missouri River near Defiance.

NADINE

The stern-wheel steamboat *Nadine* was snagged one mile above the mouth of the Missouri River on September 10, 1878, resulting in the deaths of three people. The boat and the cargo were a total loss. This could be in St. Louis County.

NEW GEORGETOWN

The side-wheel steamer *New Georgetown* was snagged and sank on May 11, 1855, at Bellefontaine Bluffs at Coldwater Creek on the Missouri River. It was headed upstream for Fort Leavenworth with U.S. government stores. No lives were lost. This could be in St. Louis County.

ST. CLAIR COUNTY

JAMES GANG CACHE

The James Gang reportedly had a hideout in a log cabin about one mile from Roscoe. They were rumored to have hidden some loot nearby.

MONTANA TREASURE

The steamboat *Montana* sank in 1843 after hitting the Wabash Bridge on the Missouri River near Hermann while carrying a reported cargo of gold bullion and mercury, according to Glenn E. Haydon's article in *Saga* magazine. Only a small part of the cargo was salvaged. Haydon thought that much treasure remained.

OLD DAVE'S TREASURE

The Dave Rock Farm was near Lowry City, off Missouri Highway 16 North. On this farm, a faithful slave named Old Dave reportedly helped cache his master's money. Kansas Jayhawkers, Confederate guerrillas, outlaws and bushwhackers roamed the area during the Civil War. Dave and his master both died without disclosing where the treasure was cached. Supposedly, this treasure has not been found. One treasure hunter reported that the farm site is very rocky, with the old house foundations reported to still be visible.

SILVER CAVE AND LOST MINE

This cave is 1,752 feet long and has a lost treasure and a lost silver mine associated with it.

ST. LOUIS COUNTY

EDNA

See St. Charles County.

FATHER DONNELLY'S TREASURE

Thomas Penfield's *A Guide to Treasure in Missouri* says that this treasure is lost in St. Louis. It actually was lost in Kansas City, Missouri. See Jackson County.

Gangster Jewelry Cache

A gang reportedly robbed a St. Louis jewelry store of $30,000 worth of items. A dying gangster claimed the jewelry was buried under an oak tree between two large roots in the Clayton area west of St. Louis. The other gangsters involved in the robbery had been killed. This area is now heavily developed with houses and other infrastructure.

Greenlease Kidnapping Ransom

One of the most infamous U.S. kidnapping cases involved the son of wealthy Cadillac car distributor Robert Greenlease Sr. On September 28, 1953, a woman claiming to be the aunt of six-year-old Robby "Bobby" Cosgrove Greenlease pulled him out of the French Institute Notre Dame de Sion School in Kansas City, Missouri. Robert Greenlease was then informed that to save his son's life he needed to pay a large ransom. While trying to avoid getting police involved, Robert paid the kidnappers a record $600,000 in $20 and $10 bills from all twelve Federal Reserve banks.

The kidnappers were Carl Austin Hall and his girlfriend, Bonnie Emily Headley. They drove Bobby Greenlease across the state line in a station wagon to a field near Overland Park, Kansas. Because the kidnappers crossed a state line, the Federal Bureau of Investigation was able to get involved. Hall murdered the young boy with a gun, and then Hall and Headley transported his body to St. Joseph, Missouri. There, Hall dug a three-by-five-foot hole in Headley's backyard garden and buried Bobby Greenlease. They planted flowers over the grave. Hall and Headley were both alcoholics. Hall, also a drug addict, was the son of a lawyer. He had gotten out of prison on April 24 and was on parole for a five-year conviction for robbing a taxicab driver of thirty-five dollars. Headley worked as a prostitute.

Hall and Headley then traveled to St. Louis. John Heidenry's *Zero at the Bone* is a well-researched book on the Greenlease kidnapping and presents a lot of information on the events. Heidenry also discusses what might have happened to the ransom money.

One popular story not in Heidenry's book claimed that while in St. Louis, Hall bought a shovel and two garbage cans. Hall rented a car, reportedly drove to the Meramec River bottoms and buried the two trash cans with about $300,000 of the cash. This story claimed that Hall was drunk when he buried the trash cans and afterward couldn't remember where he cached the money. A version on the FBI website states that Hall stayed at the Coral Courts Motel in Marlborough, left two empty trash cans in a clubhouse and later moved to an apartment in the Town House Hotel (5316 Pershing Avenue) in St. Louis. The FBI spent some time searching the Meramec River bottoms for the ransom. In 1955, mysterious diggings took place on land near Bland, Missouri, so there could be some element of truth in this version. Headley stayed at a rented St. Louis apartment at 4505 Arsenal Street after Hall left her. She appears to have spent a lot of time drunk and on drugs while he was out.

Lieutenant Louis Ira "The Shadow" Shoulders of the St. Louis Police Department (SLPD) had been a crooked cop for twenty-seven years and was a close friend of gangster Joe Costello. Ace Cab driver John Oliva Hagar had been driving Hall around St. Louis and became suspicious about his passenger. Hager worked for Costello, who owned Ace Cab.

On October 6, 1953, Hall was arrested by Shoulders and Patrolman Elmer Dolan. Although Hall claimed to be John James Byrne, he later fessed up to his real name. Hall led the two policemen to Headley at the apartment on Arsenal Street. There are a number of theories about what happened to the ransom money.

Shoulders and Dolan confiscated two suitcases (a footlocker and a suitcase), each containing about half of the remaining ransom money, and a briefcase from Hall and Headley. While Hall and Headley were being booked at the police station, Shoulders took one suitcase with ransom money and likely gave it to Costello. Joe Costello probably gave the money to other mobsters with the intention of fencing the marked currency. The bills had been marked and recorded. One version of this story has a dirty shovel being found in the apartment, indicating that part of the money might have been buried nearby. The FBI and the SLPD did not share information on the Greenlease investigations, so there was a lot of confusion in this case.

The FBI knew the SLPD was corrupt and tied to gangsters. One scenario was that the gangsters sent the money to Havana, Cuba mob casinos to launder the money. Also, the gangsters might have used traveling carnivals to launder the "hot" money. Some currency may also have been hidden. A number of people associated with the St. Louis gangsters were murdered or mysteriously disappeared.

At the trials of Hall and Headley, there was ample evidence of their guilt in the Bobby Greenlease kidnapping and murder. The couple pleaded guilty and told the police that Bobby's body was buried in Headley's flower garden in her St. Joseph house. Bloodstains were found in Headley's home and on one of her blouses. Shell casings and a bullet were recovered. A spent bullet was found in the station wagon floor that matched the .38-caliber pistol taken from Hall. On December 18, 1953, Carl Austin Hall and Bonnie Emily Headley were executed in a gas chamber in the Jefferson City Missouri Penitentiary.

The St. Louis police had a documented recovery of $295,140 ($288,000), but $301,401 ($312,000) was not accounted for, as it had been stolen or spent. The missing money was said to be 13,401 $20 bills and 3,570 $10 bills. The first recovered marked bill was from a bank in Minot, North Dakota. A total of at least 115 marked bills from the ransom were recovered, mostly in the Chicago area. This might have been some of the ransom money that Hall and Headley spent before being arrested.

The stories of what happened to the missing ransom contain many lies, half truths and misdirection. Criminals, murderers, kidnappers, dirty cops and the mob were all involved in this crime. Hall and Headley were quickly tried and executed. Hall and Headley evidently had been threatened by both the SLPD and gangsters to keep quiet. It is possible their families were threatened with harm if Hall or Headley talked too much about where the missing money went.

Lieutenant Shoulders was later arrested and sentenced to three years in prison for corruption and perjury. Joe Costello was known to have helped Shoulder's wife with money while Shoulders was in prison. Shoulders died on May 12, 1962. Dolan was also arrested and sentenced to two years in prison for perjury. He had received at least $1,500 from Joe Costello after Dolan got out of prison. In September 1962, Dolan flew to Washington, D.C., where he told the FBI that Shoulders had received half the ransom money, which he gave to Costello. President Lyndon B. Johnson pardoned Dolan on July 12, 1965, based on FBI director J. Edgar Hoover's recommendation.

Johnny Carr owned the Coral Courts Motel, where Hall had been staying while he was supposed to have been looking for a place to bury part of the ransom. Carr was involved with gangsters and might have been a party with some of the missing ransom. Carr reportedly exhibited some wealth after Hall and Headley were arrested. Carr was rumored to have stolen part of the money when Hall passed out, possibly in a room at his hotel. The hotel was later torn down, and the eight acres around it were developed as a housing subdivision.

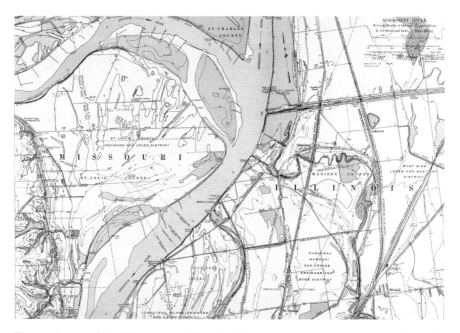

The confluence of the Missouri and Mississippi Rivers contains many shipwrecks. Some of these ships carried money. *Missouri Historical Society*.

NADINE

See St. Charles County.

NEW GEORGETOWN

Could be in St. Charles County.

OAK TREE TREASURE

A $30,000 jewelry cache was reportedly hidden in the St. Louis area.

STODDARD COUNTY

BLOOMFIELD TREASURE

The Stoddard County seat is Bloomfield. The courthouse was on a hill in the center of Bloomfield and had a Union fort built around it in the Civil War. During the war, much of the town was destroyed. Gold and silver were reportedly buried at the edge of town near a fire-gutted house with only a lone chimney remaining. No one has reported finding any treasure, although a number of Civil War artifacts have been found over the years with the use of metal detectors.

FOUND TREASURE CHEST

See Butler County.

JENKINS LOST TREASURE

An old farmer named Jenkins lived on a hog farm near Bloomfield in the 1890s. Before he died, it was thought he had buried several jars of money. Ghost hogs were said to guard his treasure cache. A lone chimney was said to have marked the site for many years. The chimney makes this story resemble the "Bloomfield Treasure."

STONE COUNTY

BALDKNOBBERS TREASURE

Baldknobbers were vigilantes formed about 1884. They were night riders who terrorized people in the Ozarks. They supposedly used a cave on Breadtray Mountain as their base and hid their loot there. Baldknobber groups were also in Christian, Douglas and Taney Counties. In 1889, all but one of the baldknobbers in this area were said to have been captured and killed.

Civil War Galena Treasure

A legend from the Civil War claimed that Confederate sympathizers hid $1 million in silver bars on the James River near Galena. The river flooded the area and reportedly destroyed the markers needed to find the treasure.

Hillary Farrington Treasure

On the old Duram farm near Jeona, Hillary Farrington's treasure was supposedly cached. This may be the same story as "Farrington Treasure," Lawrence County.

Lost Alonzus Hall Treasure

During the Civil War, bushwhacker Alonzus Hall led a number of outlaws from the Springfield, Missouri area. These bushwhackers raided along the Arkansas-Missouri border. In early April 1862, Hall and six men reportedly robbed a Missouri bank of $52,000 in gold coins. The bushwhacking band traveled south and robbed two farms. From one farm, they took $4,000; from the other, they stole $6,000. Union Captain W.F. McCullough (McCulla) led a company stationed about twenty-five miles west of Springfield, near where the Frisco Railroad was later built. McCullough's Union troops pursued the Hall Gang. The Union soldiers chased the bushwhackers through Greene, Christian and Stone Counties.

Two days after the robberies, the Union soldiers caught up with the gang, which had camped under a ledge on the bank of the White River at the old ferryboat crossing of Wilderness Road. The bushwhackers reportedly hid their cache in a cave and buried buckskin bags of loot in four different locations. It could be that each bushwhacker buried their share of the loot. They concealed the cave entrance with rocks and brush.

Union troops attacked and quickly overcame the outnumbered bushwhackers. All the outlaws but Hall were killed. Hall had a serious stomach wound. Three Union soldiers were also killed in the fight. Hall was transported by wagon to a camp on the White River near Reeds Spring. He was then taken to the Springfield Union Army hospital.

Hall was treated by a Dr. Boucher (Bushay or Busha). Hall's wound was fatal, so he told Dr. Boucher about the robberies and the caches. Boucher wrote down Hall's story, and it was put in a journal, which was found in the hospital a few years later.

The treasure cave and area of caches was reportedly near an overhanging ledge near Kimberling (Kimberly) Bridge. There was supposedly a narrow crack in the roof of the limestone cave that let in light. Table Rock Lake might cover the cave and caches today. I was unable to find the name Alonzus Hall in the official records in *The War of the Rebellion*, so it could have been an alias or part of a legend. Some stories have the robbed bank being in Centralia, but that location doesn't fit the rest of the story.

Lost Breadtray Silver Mine and Cache

According to legend, the 1,354-foot-tall Breadtray Mountain contains a lost silver mine as well as a treasure cache. Breadtray Mountain is near the James River and White River junction, which is now part of Table Rock Lake. There is a Bread Tray Mountain in St. Francois County not related to this tale. Chickasaw Indians reportedly said they had a mine in the area, from which they got silver to make jewelry. The Indians supposedly hid silver in a cave and sealed it near or on Breadtray Mountain. Spaniards who came to this area reportedly forced Indians to mine the silver for them. The Indians attacked the Spaniards, who were going to leave the area, and supposedly killed all but three, who escaped. The three Spaniards later returned for their silver and were killed.

Lost Spanish Silver Mines

Several lost Spanish mines were said to be within a five-mile radius of Galena.

Lost Yocum Mine

The Lost Yocum Mine was reportedly located between the Kings and James Rivers near present-day Table Rock Lake. Jim (James) Yocum (Yoachum) migrated from Illinois to southwestern Missouri about 1800. He had an Indian wife and settled near where the James and White Rivers join. From his Indian wife, Jim Yocum learned about a secret site where Indians had

Several lost mines are supposed to be located near or in Table Rock Lake. *Author collection.*

mined silver to make jewelry. Yocum fought in the War of 1812. Indians reportedly traded the location of their secret mine for horses in 1835, as the Indians were being chased out of the area by the U.S. government. Jim and his brother Solomon extracted silver from the mine. One story claimed that they found the mine by tracing an old trail to a ridge, where they found a cave entrance. This turned out to be a mine. Inside, they found skeletons and Spanish relics. They also found a rich silver vein.

Solomon moved his family to Missouri. The Yocums minted their silver into what was called Yocum dollars, as money was scarce. Yocum dollars were examined by government agents in Springfield and then Washington, D.C. Since the coins had "Yocum Dollar" stamped on them, the government did not consider them to be counterfeit. They were likely used as trade tokens in the area.

A mine cave-in occurred in 1846 or 1847, killing Jim and his wife. Their bodies were said to have never been recovered from the mine. Solomon Yocum and his family left Missouri for California during the gold rush about 1849. Before leaving, they concealed the mine entrance. In 1958 or 1959, a Yocum descendent (a grandson of Solomon Yocum) who had moved to California came to the area with an old map to find the mine. The map indicated that the mine was in the Breadtray Mountain area. The owner of the land where the mine was located refused to sell, so the Yocum descendant left after telling this tale. The landowner tried to find the mine but reportedly did no excavations until 1965. He was reportedly short of money and never found any great silver deposit. Several people were said to know where the mine had been.

OLD SPANISH CAVE TREASURE

Near Branson, off Missouri 160 north of Reeds Spring, is a commercial cave called Old Spanish Cave. A treasure legend is associated with it. The cave is 1,800 feet in length. An Indian claimed there was a cave with a large silver vein that four Spaniards had discovered. Three of the Spaniards died, but the fourth man sealed the cave with his companions' bodies inside. He made a map and marked trees and rocks to help him find the site in the future. People from Joplin and Reeds Spring searched for this treasure based on the old map. Old Spanish Cave was reportedly discovered in 1892 using the old Spanish map. Inside the cave were skeletons, decayed blankets, artifacts, pottery, pictographs, an old copper cup and other items. Despite the cave having been explored, no treasure was ever known to have been recovered. Later, moonshine was made in the cave, and it became a commercial cave in 1924.

PARSON KEITHY'S GOLD

Parson Keithy was a wandering preacher who preached on Sundays and spent a lot of time hunting with his trusty dog. When he received news of the California Gold Rush, Keithy left his family in Missouri to try his luck mining gold. He was gone for three years and returned to his place in Missouri with $5,000 ($8,000) in gold in 1850s value. This would be worth about $250,000 today. He hid his gold but did not disclose its location to his family. He was said to occasionally pull a $10 gold piece out of his pocket and exclaim to his daughter, "See what I've found." He often visited a cave near Galena that became known as Keithy's Cave. Keithy planned to be buried in his cave after he died, so he blocked off part of the cave to create a mausoleum. It had foot-high wall of rocks with a double door that he could shut. He reportedly died when he was ninety. Some think he hid the gold in the cave, but family members reportedly said it was likely hidden in their garden or near an apple tree a distance from his house. This could be in Taney County.

SPANISH LEAD MINE

About eighteen miles southwest of Galena, seven Spaniards mined silver while working in a lead mine. Galena is an area where much lead mining took place. The Spaniards refined the silver ore and cached it in a cave about one mile from the mine. A dispute among the miners developed into a fight from which only Pedro Diego survived. Diego later had two Irishman partners, Higgins and McCabe. Diego was said to have disappeared, and the two Irishmen went to Boston with the refined silver. Watson Johnson, a Vermont farmer, was later found dead at the mouth of the mine shaft. This is probably a story about a lead and zinc mine with a little silver associated with it.

SPANISH TRADER TREASURE

See Taney County.

SULLIVAN COUNTY

GANGSTER CACHES

Fred "Killer" Burke was a notorious murderer, robber and gangster who may have been part of the St. Valentine's Day Massacre. On February 14, 1929, seven people in a rival gang or associated with a rival gang were murdered in a Lincoln Park garage in Chicago. Al Capone's henchmen reportedly did the shooting. Burke was involved in many murders, robberies and other crimes. Among his many aliases were Fred Dean, Fred Campbell, Theordore Cameron, Fred White, Richard F. White and Fred Dane. He was born Thomas A. Camp in Mapleton, Kansas, on May 29, 1893, but changed his name to Fred Burke after being involved in criminal activity and the law looking for Thomas Camp.

Fred was said to have obtained $100,000 from robberies and other criminal acts. He tried to have a normal life and married a farmer's daughter, Bonnie Porter, in Green City. He lived on the Green City farm and traveled as a salesman, according to his wife. It was said that he divided his $100,000 into five parcels. He kept one parcel of cash to live off of but hid the rest.

While in Michigan supposedly buying farm equipment, he was stopped by a policeman. In a panic, Fred shot and killed the policeman and fled the state.

He was later recognized and reported to the police, who arrested him. His wife claimed that she did not know he was a criminal and murderer. Fred Burke was tried and sentenced to life in prison. He died in prison on July 10, 1940.

TANEY COUNTY

ALF BOLIN'S TREASURE

A Confederate guerrilla band in Southwest Missouri was led by sixteen-year-old bushwhacker Alfred "Alf" Bolin (Bolan, Bowlan, Bolen, Boler, Boldon and Bowling in various reports and stories). Many sources indicate that Bolin was not really a Confederate guerrilla leader but a bushwhacker and murderer during the Civil War. There were many other guerrillas in Southeast Missouri named Bolin who are not part of this treasure story. Alf Bolin may have been a relative of one of these Bolins.

One interesting story claimed that Alf Bolin killed his pro-Union foster father and then fled to become a professional killer. Other stories say that he was orphaned when he was young and became extremely violent. Alf Bolin's hunting grounds were throughout Taney and Christian Counties in Missouri and Northwest Arkansas. Bolin and his gang killed boys as young as twelve and men as old as eighty. He often tortured his prey. Alf reportedly killed between fourteen and forty men after robbing them of their money. One legend claimed that he hid his loot in the Fox Creek area near the Missouri-Arkansas border on the Missouri side.

Murder Rocks (Murder Rock) and Bolin Rocks are on the old Springfield-Harrison Road in Section 25, Township 22, Range 21. Murder Rocks was a well-known limestone outcrop where robbers often hid and ambushed travelers between Springfield, Missouri, and Harrison, Arkansas. At Murder Rocks, Alf Bolin robbed a U.S. mail carrier from Harrison, Arkansas, heading to Forsyth. Two Union soldiers on furlough were also said to have been ambushed and murdered by Bolin at Murder Rocks.

Murder Rocks is now only about sixty feet east of a modern road called Murder Rock Road Trail in the Buffalo Ridge development, close to the Buffalo Ridge Golf Club and Murder Rock Golf Club. Murder Rocks is located about four miles south of Branson and within the boundaries of the town of Hollister.

Many Union expeditions went into the Ozark Mountains hunting for Alf Bolin and his gang. Bolin knew the area well and had several hiding places.

A Confederate soldier named Foster had been captured by Union forces and wanted to make a deal for his freedom. Foster's home was said to have been about three miles south of Murder Rocks, near old Layton Mill. A Union soldier, Zachariah E. Thomas of the First Iowa Cavalry Regiment, volunteered to set a trap to kill or capture Bolin. Thomas was a Missourian, although he was in the Iowa regiment.

Foster reported that Alf Bolin often dined at the Foster home, as he usually camped nearby. Some people believed that Bolin hid his loot near this campsite. The Union troops made a deal to release Foster if his wife allowed Zachariah Thomas to stay at the Fosters' home and kill or capture Bolin. Foster agreed. Thomas disguised himself as a sick Confederate soldier and went to Foster's home.

Mrs. Foster pretended to be tending to Zachariah Thomas to help him recover from his sickness so that he could return home. Alf Bolin arrived at the Fosters' house on February 2, 1863. After a discussion with Thomas, Bolin believed Thomas's story. There are several versions of what happened next. The most likely story is that as Bolin sat down to eat, Thomas hit him over the head with a broken plowshare or fireplace poker, killing Bolin. Thomas then hit Bolin again until he was sure Bolin was dead. Another version has Thomas stabbing Bolin to death in front of the fireplace as Bolin was bending over the fire to light his pipe.

Union soldiers waiting nearby came to the house and put Bolin's body onto a cart. The soldiers had so much trouble transporting Bolin's body north over rough ground that they cut Bolin's head off and put it in a box for ease of transport. Bolin's body was then quickly buried in a ditch beside the road before the soldiers continued their trip to Ozark. At Ozark, the Union soldiers reportedly put Bolin's head on a pole to display it as a warning to bushwhackers and robbers. They also wanted to prove that the hated Alf Bolin was dead.

Thomas was likely the same Lieutenant Zachariah E. Thomas who later was in charge of Company E of the Union Eleventh Missouri Cavalry Regiment that went on a scouting expedition against Confederate guerrillas in Arkansas in 1864. He may have gotten the promotion to lieutenant for killing Bolin. Thomas may have also received a reward for killing Bolin.

Supposedly, Bolin's gang claimed Alf Bolin hid his treasure of silver and gold near Bolin's Cave. This cave was in the Fox Creek Hills region, near Section 20, Township 22, Range 20 in Taney County, Missouri. Other sources claimed that Bolin Cave is about two miles southwest of the Old Mincy Store and Mill. There is in fact a Bolin Cave, open to the public, near Ozark. I believe that this is not the same cave as the one mentioned in this treasure story.

Many years after the Civil War, an old man came to Taney County to hunt for a certain cave in the hills. The man stayed several summers off and on with a farm family. The family learned from the old man that he had a Bolin treasure map and that Bolin Cave was a key to finding the treasure. The farmer's family originally believed the old man was looking for lead and zinc deposits, as several lead and zinc mines were nearby. Finally, the man left and never came back. The family didn't believe that the old man had located Bolin's treasure.

SPANISH TRADER TREASURE

A Spanish trader supposedly cached $3 million near Branson. This could be in Stone County.

SPANISH PERUVIAN TREASURE AND LOST MINE

See Douglas County.

TEXAS COUNTY

LICKING TREASURE

A large treasure was rumored to have been hidden in the hills above Licking, which was about one-quarter mile from an old buffalo lick near the head of Spring Creek. John Baldridge and Barney Low settled in Licking in 1826. The treasure may have been hidden in a cave near Spring Creek. Indians could have cached the treasure. It was said that as late as 1899 Indians visited the cave.

OUTLAW LOOKOUT TOWER TREASURE

A man known as Harry Watson was actually robber Henry Getchie. He had a house and outbuildings that he had upgraded. He also built an eighty-foot-tall wooden lookout tower on his property around 1930. The tower became known as the Outlaw Lookout Tower after he was arrested for mail theft. Getchie was convicted and later died in prison. There were rumors that he hid his loot on his property and that it was never found.

WARNER COUNTY

FOUND COINS

See Gasconade County.

WASHINGTON COUNTY

BIG RIVER CACHE

In 1971, several people arrived at an area south of Shirley on the upper headwaters of Big River (a Meramec River tributary) looking for a certain rock with a turkey track and two slashes carved into it. The rock was the key to the location of a buried barrel containing money. Reportedly, they did not find the marker. The treasure is still lost. This could be in Jefferson County.

MERAMEC RIVER TREASURES

See Franklin County.

WILLIAM SILVEY TREASURE

William Silvey and his family lived just north of the community of Shirley after the Civil War. William had come to the area from Tennessee or Ohio. William supposedly buried a metal bucket containing silver coins. He never told his family where he hid his cache. He was considered a rich man, as he owned a general store and a farm. William suffered a stroke, which affected his speech and kept him confined to bed. He was unable to communicate with his wife when she asked him where his treasure was hidden. Finally, Mrs. Silvey thought she heard him say "penitentiary," but she could not figure out what it meant. William reportedly pointed out a window. After a long illness, he died. William Silvey's son or nephew came to the area in 1921 to search for the lost treasure. He talked to old-timers in an attempt to get information on where the treasure was located. Finally, an old-timer recalled that a nearby valley was called Penitentiary Hollow, with Penitentiary Creek running through it. Silvey's relative searched for a while but never found any treasure.

WAYNE COUNTY

HAUNTED HOUSE TREASURE

At a haunted house at Taskee (Tuskee, Taskee Station), a cache of gold and silver coins was reportedly hidden. Taskee was a little community on Otter Creek, just east of Williamsville. An old farmer was reportedly murdered for his hidden money there. One townsperson reportedly did find some treasure there, but there might have been other caches.

JESSE JAMES GADS HILL LOOT

Gads Hill was a flag station on the Iron Mountain Railroad between Des Arc and Piedmont. It was named after author Charles Dickens's country home, Gads Hill. Jesse James and four outlaws (likely Frank James, Arthur McCoy, Jim Younger and John Younger) from the James-Younger Gang rode into Gads Hill on January 31, 1874. They took seven or eight men prisoner and held them in the station. This was reportedly the entire male population of Gads Hill, as the community had a total population of just fifteen people. A signal flag was put out, instructing the train coming from St. Louis to stop. The outlaws climbed onto the stopped train and entered the passenger coaches to rob the occupants. They also robbed the express car. The gang's haul from the robbery was reported

Frank James survived many robberies and gunfights. Although never convicted, he was under surveillance the rest of his life. *Library of Congress.*

by several sources to be between $2,000 and $22,000. Also stolen were a gold watch, five handguns, a ring and a diamond stickpin. The robbers reportedly looked at the male passengers' hands to determine if they were working men or gentlemen. They only robbed the gentlemen and did not rob the ladies on the train. This was the first train robbery in Missouri.

A posse of twenty-five men went after the robbers the next day. A snowstorm helped the posse track the outlaws. They found the trail where the gang had crossed the Black River about six miles northwest of Gads Hill and had taken the Lesterville Road north. The trail led to Three Forks, and on the Middle Fork the posse found a worn-down horse that the outlaws had stolen from one of the posse members from Gads Hill. The posse continued to track the outlaws but halted. The gang headed into Reynolds County and crossed the Current River and then split up, with the James boys going to their family's farm in Clay County.

Several different areas were said to be where loot from this robbery was cached. One was an area in the hills east of the robbery, where the outlaws lightened the load of their horses as they were escaping. Two of the robbers, John and Jim Younger, were tracked down by detectives. On March 17, 1874, detectives Louis J. Lull and John Boyle and Deputy Sheriff Edwin B. Daniels got into a gunfight with the fugitives. Daniels, Lull and John Younger were killed on a Missouri road near Roscoe.

In September 1948, a woodcutter reported finding a cave in a hill. Wild stories about the woodcutter recovering $100,000 in coins and currency spread through the countryside. Newspaper reporters tracked him down, and the woodcutter claimed that he had recovered a rusty rifle, a book and a few two-cent pieces (one dated 1886) from the cave, but nothing else. The *St. Louis Globe-Democrat* reported that no Jesse James treasure was found by the woodcutter.

Wright County

Lost Gold Mine

A lost gold mine was reportedly located somewhere in Wright County.

Spanish Cave Treasure

Spanish Cave on the Norfolk River was said to contain a hidden cache of $800,000 in gold coins.

Unknown County

Forty Jack Loads of Gold

A legend claimed that somewhere in Southwest Missouri, Spaniards forced Indians to mine silver in an old Indian silver mine. The Indians revolted, so the Spaniards took refuge in the mine with forty jack loads of gold that was intended to be sent east. The Indians closed the mine entrance, killing the Spaniards.

Found Bucket of Gold

John Hankins had a farm in a valley in the Ozarks. He and his wife were successful. John did not tell his wife where he cached their gold pieces. One day, a mule kicked John in the head in the barn. When his wife found him on the ground, he was in bad shape and dying. He reportedly pointed to the well and the yard and mumbled, "money," before dying.

Mrs. Hankins ran the farm with the help of her family and friends after her husband's death. One of her brothers visited her with his two young sons. They were playing in the barn when they accidentally knocked into an old bucket, which fell off the barn wall to the ground and broke. A false bottom was revealed, and more than twenty-four twenty-dollar gold pieces spilled out.

Found Silver Bullion

Robert L. Tatham's *Missouri Treasures and Civil War Sites* has a story about a man using a metal detector in 1969 on a farm once owned by his granduncle, who was said to have been a miser who didn't trust banks or paper currency. This granduncle reportedly had a hoard of gold coins worth about $20,000 that he sold in the 1930s for silver when the United States went off the gold standard and it became illegal to own gold except for jewelry and other items. The man with the metal detector hit the jackpot and found a tin box containing ten silver bars on the property in the old vegetable garden. The ten bars were not worth $20,000, so there was a question as to whether additional silver had been hidden by the granduncle.

House Fire Gold Coins

Tatham's book tells the story of another treasure hunter who had a metal detector. He wanted to use it to check out an old house. After many delays, he arrived at the site of the old house and discovered it had burned down. He used his metal detector at the site and found thirty-one five-dollar gold pieces that had been hidden in the house.

Mr. J's Cache of Silver Coins

Treasure hunter and writer Robert L. Tatham heard several stories from different sources about a Mr. J who had hidden $1,000 or more in coins before he died around 1900. Tatham's family had hunted unsuccessfully for this cache over the years before metal detectors became available. Tatham hunted for the cache for three hours one day and found lots of junk iron and old zinc lids for jars. On the second day, he got a signal and dug to another zinc lid when he discovered the lid was on top of a half-gallon glass jar. After digging around the jar, he lifted it out of the ground. It looked at first like a jar full of gold coins, due to the tint of the jar. The jar turned out to contain eighty-four silver dollars from the 1880s. Whether Mr. J had other caches is not known.

2

MINING

The Ozark Uplift is a region of carbonate rocks located in Missouri and Northwest Arkansas that contained various mineral deposits, especially lead and zinc. Indians mined flint and other minerals before Europeans came to Missouri. Some Indians located mineral deposits and used bright minerals and crystals as lucky charms or talismans. These minerals were often traded with other tribes. Osage Indians used lead from some deposits to make musket bullets. It is also likely that Chickasaw Indians and other tribes mined lead.

When Missouri was part of French Louisiana, the La Motte Mining District was discovered in Southeast Missouri in 1717 by Frenchman M. La Motte near present-day Fredericktown in Madison County. The Company of the West, a French firm, secured mining rights from the French king in this area. French and Spanish prospectors discovered lead in what later became the Tri-State Mining District of Southwest Missouri, Northwest Arkansas and Southeast Kansas.

Kaskaskia, Illinois, and the French forts on the east bank of the Mississippi River were staging areas for prospectors looking for valuable minerals in Missouri. About 1735, the town of Ste. Genevieve was founded in Missouri as a base for lead miners to process ore and to extract salt from Saline Creek. Later, the town was moved to higher ground due to Mississippi River floods covering the town every few years.

French and Spanish explorers and miners found mineral deposits throughout the Ozark region. The Mississippi River and its vast tributaries

Ste. Genevieve was established about 1735 by the French as a Missouri mining and prospecting base. *Author collection.*

were the highways of commerce, as roads were in poor shape and were for the most part Indian trails. Any mined minerals would be floated downstream, mainly to New Orleans, where they could be transported by oceangoing vessels to Europe or other parts of the Americas. Neither France nor Spain had extensive funding for exploration and development of the vast Louisiana Territory, due to their global wars.

Part of French Louisiana became a Spanish territory under the Treaty of Paris of February 10, 1763, as a result of major French defeats in the Americas. Under Spanish rule, St. Louis became a center of lead exports from what is now Missouri. About 17,800 pounds of lead were taken through St. Louis in 1773. Under the Treaty of San Ildefonso of 1800, France was granted its former territory of Louisiana. French Emperor Napoleon Bonaparte needed money and sold Louisiana to the United States in 1803 for $15 million. France was battling a number of European countries and needed to pay for soldiers, weapons and ships.

Lead in this region was often found as galena, a lead sulfide that forms cube crystals. Ore was mined from the surface to about four hundred feet or more in depth. Small amounts of silver and other minerals were often found with the lead. Zinc in the form of sphalerite was often associated with lead.

Several lost mines are said to be located in the area of the scenic White River in Southwest Missouri and Northwest Arkansas. Man-made lakes now exist on the White River for water supply, electric generation, flood control and recreation. These lakes include Lake Taneycomo, Bull Shoals Lake, Table Rock Lake and Beaver Lake. Rivers and streams often follow faults and fractured rocks containing minerals.

About 1819, Henry Schoolcraft traveled through Missouri and Arkansas in search of mineral deposits. In 1819, he published *A View of the Lead Mines of Missouri*. Schoolcraft reported seeing ancient mining works on the bank of the White River near Bull Shoals buried under fifteen to twenty feet of soil. He found pieces of metallic lead and earthen pots in these early works. This early mining site may be near or under Bull Shoals Lake in Marion County, Arkansas. Another indication of mining in the Ozarks is an 1822 map showing a lead mine on the White River.

One estimate claimed that between 1803 and 1819, about fifty-five million pounds of Missouri lead had been smelted. One report said that the Washington County area in 1822 contained three-three to forty-five mines, including Mine La Motte, Mine a Breton and others. The rights to mines became a subject of conflict over time. Some mining took place on public lands, and many people thought that mining should be open to all who claimed a site where they discovered minerals. Others had grants from France or Spain and believed the United States should honor those title transfers. Many areas saw litigation for decades over land titles.

In the 1840s, lead mining by Americans began in southwestern Missouri. By the Civil War, Jasper and Newton Counties had many mines and mining camps on Shoal Creek and elsewhere. The mines provided much of the lead for bullets in the early part of the war, but raids by both sides, devastation of the area and depopulation resulted in the mines being closed down during much of the war.

In the 1870s, large mines were established near Joplin and other areas. Large zinc deposits were discovered, and Missouri became one of the largest areas of lead and zinc mining in the world. Zinc production peaked in 1916. The Tri-State Mining District was the largest producer of lead and zinc concentrates in the world for a time. From 1875 to 1950, 50 percent of U.S.-produced lead and zinc came from this district. By 1957, the Southwest Missouri lead and zinc mines had been exhausted or were uneconomical, so mining stopped.

Silver production in Missouri has been a byproduct of lead and zinc mining and refining. In the 1950s, it was reported that two ounces of silver

Missouri lead was refined in mills like this one. *State Historical Society of Missouri.*

Mine chat piles were used for road material. Few remain to mark old mines. *State Historical Society of Missouri.*

were recovered per ton of refined pig lead. From 1905 to 1965, more than 8.7 million ounces of silver were mined in Missouri. Most of the silver came from the Bonne Terre formation as a result of lead and zinc mining. In some areas of the lead belt, almost 25.0 ounces of silver were refined per ton of lead (galena) and zinc (sphalerite). In the Tri-State Mining District, silver was reported to average about 0.1 ounce per ton.

Only the Einstein Mine and surrounding areas in Madison County were mined primarily for silver. Silver had been mined in this area since 1879 but in a limited capacity. These silver veins were in granite. One vein reportedly resulted in fifty tons of lead and three thousand ounces of silver.

There have been no reports of economic quantities of gold ever being mined in Missouri. Some small gold flakes have been found in glacier deposits in Northeast Missouri. In the early days, iron sulfide—"fool's gold"—was sometimes mistaken for gold.

3

LOST MINES

As a French colony and later the Spanish colony of Louisiana Territory, Missouri was explored for wealth by many expeditions. Tales of French and Spanish lost mines were left behind as part of that legacy. Early explorers discovered much evidence of Missouri's minerals in their travels.

There was indeed much untapped mineral wealth in Missouri in the geologic region called the Ozark Uplift. Undoubtedly, early prospectors and miners faced many obstacles during the frontier times. Hostile Indians and disease claimed a number of early prospectors and miners who had found riches in the ground.

When settlers moved into Missouri, they often found evidence of early mining from piles of debris, holes in the ground and markings on rocks and trees. There were stories of French and Spanish miners finding gold and silver in the Ozarks, and these stories were then passed down over the generations. Lead deposits seem often to have been mistaken for silver deposits.

Southwest Missouri and adjacent Northwest Arkansas share what seem to be similar legends of early Spanish mining expeditions finding rich mines but being driven from the area. An "Old Spanish Cave" is located in both Arkansas and Missouri and seems to be the subject of the same or a very similar story.

Many valuable minerals were located during European exploration, but as discussed in chapter 2, these sites were not exploited until roads and infrastructure became available. Most of the minerals were near large waterways, such as those found in southeastern and eastern Missouri. Minerals located in southwestern Missouri were mined later than those near the Mississippi River in eastern Missouri.

Lost Missouri mine tales are the following: Indian Eagle Rock Mine and Cave, Barry County; Indian Silver Mine, Barry County; Indian Silver Mine and Cache, Barry County; Lost Chickasaw Mine, Barry County; White River Mines, Barry County; Lost Indian Mine, Carter County and Wright County; Lost Carpenter Creek Gold Mine, Cedar County; Lost Missouri Mine, Dallas County and Camden County; Spanish Peruvian Treasure and Lost Mine, Douglas County, Ozark County and Taney County; Lost Spanish and French Mines, Greene County; Lost Brooksie Silver Mine, Hickory County; Lost Silver Mine, Jefferson County; Lost Sugar River Gold Mine, McDonald County; Splitlog Mine and Cache, McDonald County; Lost Louisiana Mine, Montgomery County; Noble Hill Spanish Mine, Polk County; Limonite Gold, Pulaski County; Black River Silver Mine, Reynold County; Slater's Lost Mine Found, Shannon County; Lost Silver Cave and Mine, St. Clair County; Lost Breadtray Silver Mine and Cache, Stone County; Lost Spanish Silver Mines, Stone County; Lost Yocum Mine, Stone County; Spanish Lead Mine, Stone County; and Lost Gold Mine, Wright County.

4

EXPLORERS, TRADERS
AND MIGRANTS

Explorers, traders and migrants going west used Missouri's waterways to cross into the American frontier. The Mississippi and Missouri Rivers were relatively easy to navigate, compared to going overland on Indian trails.

St. Louis became a giant center for traders, trappers, migrants and shippers during Missouri's early years. St. Louis was the center of the rich fur trade in the West. Pelts from trappers and traders were assembled in St. Louis and put onto keelboats in the early years of the trade. Later, furs were put onto steamboats. The furs were usually taken downriver to New Orleans and then were sent to worldwide markets. Some furs were also taken to Canada and sold. Lead from the Spanish mines below Dubuque, Iowa, was also transported down the Mississippi River, as were agricultural goods, to St. Louis. St. Louis grew from a town of about 637 in 1773 to a small city of 10,099 people in 1820 and then to a booming metropolis of 351,189 in 1870.

The Santa Fe Trail from Missouri to Mexican Santa Fe in present-day New Mexico was a road to riches for traders for many years. The trail was part of a route originally traveled by men such as Pedro Viel, a Frenchman who often worked for the Spanish government. Viel took trade goods from Santa Fe to St. Louis in 1792, when both cities were under Spanish control and there were no international boundaries to cross.

After Missouri became part of the United States, American traders were generally barred from trade with the Spanish lands in present-day New

This bullboat and smaller craft also traveled Missouri rivers. A number of these craft likely sank with valuable cargo. *Missouri Historical Society.*

Mexico and elsewhere. When Mexico became independent from Spain in 1821, U.S. trade was opened up with the new nation. There were old Indian, French and Spanish trails between New Mexico and Missouri, but William Becknell pioneered a trail from Franklin on the Missouri River that was wide enough for wagons to use. Becknell journeyed from Missouri to Santa Fe in order to trade. He traded $300 worth of Missouri merchandise carried on three wagons for $6,000 in coinage and started active trading along the Missouri frontier.

In 1839, Don José Chavez and five Mexican nobles and their servants went up the Santa Fe Trail with $60,000 in coins and bought supplies in Independence and St. Louis that they then carted back to Mexico. In the spring of 1841, a twenty-two-wagon trading caravan carried about $200,000 in coins with Mexicans heading up the Santa Fe Trail for Missouri to buy supplies. The caravan returned successfully to Santa Fe without a major incident. The expedition returned with thirty-eight full wagons carrying seventy-two tons of supplies purchased in Missouri.

The murder of Don Antonio José Chavez in 1843 caused an international incident between the United States and Mexico on the frontier. The murder halted trade between the two nations for a time. This halt in trade seriously hurt Missouri-based traders and merchants, who had grown prosperous because of the Mexican trade.

In 1849, José Francisco Chavez, the brother of the murdered Don Antonio José Chavez, traveled on the Santa Fe Trail with reportedly $100,000 in Mexican silver to buy needed goods from Missouri merchants. He was joined by freighter Francis X. Aubry and his men, who convinced Chavez to trade in Westport rather than with merchants in Independence. This decision helped turn what became Kansas City into a large city.

Migrants heading to California, Oregon and Washington traveled through Missouri with their worldly belongings and their money. After the Mexican-American War, New Mexico, Arizona, California, Utah and other areas became part of the United States. Migrants and traders traveled through Missouri and often carried large sums of cash to buy horses, wagons, food and other items needed for the journey west. The discovery of gold in California in 1849 caused a vast migration of gold seekers for many years, and many of them traveled through Missouri. The discovery of gold in Montana caused another gold rush. In this case, transportation was often done by steamboat up the Missouri River. Some of the migrants returning east with their gold and silver never made it back. It is likely that some of the travelers' cash was buried along the way and not recovered.

Treasures associated with these routes in Missouri are the following: Migrating Indian Cache, Benton County; Lost Spanish Treasure, Christian County; Missouri River Lost Kettle of French Gold, Clarion County; Chavez Owens Landing Treasure, Jackson County; Migrant Train Cache, Johnson County; California Miner's Gold, Laclede County; Mark Twain Cave Treasures, Marion County and Rallis County; Spanish Miners Bear Hollow Gold, McDonald County; Spanish Jewelry, Newton County; Turkey Creek Spanish Treasure, Newton County; and Spanish Trader Treasure, Taney County and Stone County.

5

CIVIL WAR

Before the American Civil War, battles and raids in western Missouri and eastern Kansas following the passage of the Kansas-Nebraska Act in 1854 set the stage for the mayhem that followed. This war over slavery included the murders and deaths of about two hundred men on the border. During the Civil War, Missouri was a divided border state, with its citizens fighting in both armies. Rebel guerrilla bands were called partisan rangers, bushwhackers and outlaws. These guerrilla bands ranged throughout southern and central Missouri. Union raiders such as the Kansas Red Legs and other groups also raided farms and towns. A raid led by Colonel Charles Ransford Jennison consisting of forty-five Jayhawkers from his Kansas regiment and several hundred Union Missouri Militia men raided Morristown, Missouri, in July 1861. There, they murdered two civilians and stole $2,000 worth of goods, which were taken back to Kansas and distributed as booty among the Union men. A Jayhawker raid on Harrisonville resulted in the theft of much booty, including the safe of the Cass County sheriff. Money, livestock, food, furniture and everything that could be carted off by horse, mule or wagon were taken from homes throughout Missouri. Often, soldiers and outlaws robbed people on both sides during the war. Sometimes, thieves wore Union uniforms, Confederate uniforms or civilian clothes.

Colonel William Quantrill led a band of between 350 and 450 Confederate guerrillas. They crossed into Kansas from Missouri and sacked Lawrence on August 21, 1863. The guerrillas killed and murdered 150 to 180 men

Loot from William Quantrill's Confederate raid on Lawrence, Kansas, was carried to Missouri. It is likely that some of it was hidden. *New York Public Library.*

and boys, mostly civilians. Quantrill and his men robbed Lawrence of every valuable item they could carry on horseback, including money and jewelry. Lawrence was burning when they rode out of town to return to Missouri; 182 buildings were destroyed. Confederate guerrillas looted and murdered many Union soldiers and civilians in Missouri, Kansas, the Indian nations and Texas during the Civil War. Quantrill's deeds served as the training ground for future outlaws after the war. Frank and Jesse James and the Younger brothers rode with Quantrill during the Civil War.

Union Major General Thomas Ewing Jr.'s General Order No. 11 was issued on August 25, 1863, after William Quantrill's attack and burning of Lawrence, Kansas. This act ordered all residents, with some exceptions, of Bates County, Cass County, Jackson County and the north half of Vernon County to move outside of the Missouri District of the Border. These counties are close to Kansas. This order devastated Confederate families and depopulated the area until after the Civil War. Many houses were burned down and farms destroyed. More than twenty thousand people were forced to become refugees. This area was targeted, as many of the Confederate guerrillas had families there, and these families provided food and support to the guerrillas. The mandatory evacuation order was in retaliation for the looting and burning of Lawrence by William Quantrill and his guerrillas from mostly that region of Missouri.

My cousins had several of their ancestors taken prisoner in their field near Toadsuck (Leora), Missouri. A Union soldier had been killed in the area, and five Union soldiers came to the farm and murdered the two unarmed farmers in retaliation. My wife's family in Arkansas had money stolen during the Civil War from a sick relative who was lying on top of about $300 when Union soldiers entered the house. Memories of Civil War atrocities and crimes still haunt many people even today.

Confederate Major General Sterling "Pap" Price invaded Missouri on August 29, 1864, with a goal of capturing St. Louis. His army was turned back at Fort Davison in southeastern Missouri. Price's Confederate army headed for Jefferson City but was unable to approach it. The Confederates then marched west, planning to capture Kansas City and Fort Leavenworth, but again were turned back and forced to retreat south. Price's invasion ended on December 2. This invasion or raid caused much chaos among the people in Missouri. Many people hid their money, fearing robbery by Confederate guerrillas and soldiers and by bushwhackers taking the opportunity to rob.

On September 27, 1864, Captain William "Bloody Bill" Anderson led about 80 Confederate guerrillas into Centralia. They stopped a North

The Missouri Home Guard opposed Major General Sterling Price's Confederate invasion. Many Unionists hid their money or had it stolen during Price's invasion. *State Historical Society of Missouri.*

Missouri Railroad train carrying 125 passengers by blocking the tracks. The guerrillas stole $3,000 from the baggage car (express car) safe and reportedly $10,000 from the passengers. Several male passengers were murdered by the guerrillas when they were found to have hidden money and a gold watch in their boots. The guerrillas ordered the Union soldiers to remove their uniforms. The 24 defenseless soldiers were lined up and executed, except for a sergeant, whom the guerrillas planned to exchange for one of their captured guerrillas. The Union soldiers on the train were on leave following the Battle of Atlanta. The guerrillas set the train on fire as it rolled down the tracks out of town, and they burned the depot.

Major Andrew Vern Emen Johnson led three companies of the Thirty-Ninth Missouri Infantry Regiment (Mounted), consisting of about 146 men, through Centralia in pursuit of the Confederate guerrillas. Bloody Bill Anderson and his men turned to confront the Union force. Major Johnson ordered his mounted men to dismount and fight on foot with muskets against a guerrilla force on horses and armed with three or more revolvers per man. After losing several killed and wounded in their charge of the Union line, the guerrillas broke through the line, shooting Union soldiers who did not have time to reload. Anderson and his men shot and killed 123 Union soldiers and wounded 1; the guerrillas lost 3 killed and 10 wounded. Many of the Union soldiers were shot as they fled on foot. A young Jesse James was said to have killed Major Johnson during the battle.

Quantrill and his guerrillas robbed the Bank of Thompson and Dunnica in Glasgow on October 17, 1864, of about $26,000. Bank co-owner W.F. Dunnica reportedly had just hidden another $34,000, so Quantrill didn't steal that.

On October 18, Confederate guerrilla Bill Anderson captured wealthy Union Colonel Benjamin W. Lewis in Glasgow. Lewis had previously offered a $6,000 reward for the capture or killing of Anderson. Anderson brutally beat Lewis and threatened to kill him unless he gave Anderson $5,000 in gold coins. Lewis managed to raise the sum from his family and friends and was released. Lewis suffered severe injuries that led to his death a year and a half later. Anderson was shot in the head and killed on October 26 or 27 at Orrick or Albany, Missouri, by a detachment of about 150 soldiers under Lieutenant Colonel Samuel P. Cox. The Union soldiers found gold coins hidden in Anderson's money belt.

By the end of the Civil War, many southern Missouri counties had been largely depopulated. In some places, only a stone chimney marked where a home or store once stood. The small community of Sherwood and eleven

This Missouri home with several Union soldiers was typical of a prosperous family during the Civil War. *Library of Congress.*

nearby farmhouses were burned down by Union forces after the Battle of Sherwood. The homes were burned down in retaliation for Confederate Major Tom Livingston's men, who had defeated a Union foraging party. The Union party had been instructed to take everything they could carry from the farms and houses in the area. Livingston's guerrillas caught the foragers at Mrs. Radnor's farm and killed a number of them. The Union forces returned to Mrs. Radner's farm and murdered a Mr. John Bishop, a civilian. They placed his body and the bodies of ten dead Union soldiers of the First Kansas Colored Infantry Regiment who had been left behind on the previous day's battlefield inside Mrs. Radner's house and burned it to the ground.

The City of Carthage served as the center of Union operations against Confederate guerrillas in Jasper County. When the town was evacuated briefly by Union forces in October 1863, Confederate guerrillas burned down the only two brick buildings in Carthage, the county courthouse and the Carthage Academy, which served as fortified Union posts. On September 22, 1864, when Union forces again left town during Price's

These Civil War refugees in St. Louis show how little refugees often had when they escaped with their lives. *Author collection.*

Missouri invasion, Confederates again invaded Carthage and burned down the rest of the town. Jasper County, which had a population of 6,883 residents in 1860 according to the census, had only 30 residents in a December 1865 survey.

People who had cash in the border areas ravaged by both Confederate and Union forces as well as by outlaws hid their money in caches, usually in or near their homes. Some of these people were murdered, died of disease or were unable to return to retrieve their caches during the Civil War. Banks were few and were not federally protected against robbery. Banks were often robbed or taken over.

Civil War Missouri treasures include the following: White Oak Hill Guerrilla Gold, Bates County; Bollinger Treasure, Cape Girardeau County and Bollinger County; Church Hollow Treasure, Cedar County; Meramec River Treasure, Franklin County and Dallas County; Nobel Hill Treasure, Greene County and Polk County; Bushwhacker's Loot, Howell County; Colonel Porter's Treasure, Howell County; Father Donnelly's Treasure, Jackson County and St. Louis County; Confederate Treasure, Jasper County; Tom Livingston's Cache, Jasper County; Quantrill's Treasure, Laclede County; Stage Station Treasure, Lafayette County; Mark Twain Cave Treasures, Marion County and Rallis County; Charleston Treasure, Mississippi County; Treasure of the Steamer *Ruth*, Mississippi County; Hickman Treasure, Newton County; Tilley Farm Cache, Pulaski County; Old Dave's Treasure, St. Clair County; Bloomfield Treasure, Stoddard County; Civil War Galena Treasure, Stone County; Lost Alonzus Hall Treasure, Stone County; and Alf Bolin's Treasure, Taney County.

6

OUTLAWS AND THEIR LOOT

R iver pirates were said to have looted keelboats and other vessels on the Mississippi River traveling to and from ports and landings. One of the most prolific outlaw gangs after the Civil War was the James Gang, led by Jesse James and his brother Frank. The brothers had ridden with William Quantrill during the Civil War. The Younger brothers were occasional members of the James Gang, and it was then called the James-Younger Gang. Frank Triplett's *The Life, Times & Treacherous Death of Jesse James* tabulated $263,278 stolen by the James Gang in robberies from 1866 to 1881 from twenty train, bank and stagecoach robberies.

The James Gang was credited by Frank Triplett in his book with the following Missouri robberies: Liberty on January 20, 1866 ($72,000); Richmond in 1867 ($4,000); Gallatin on December 7, 1869 ($700); Kansas City Fair on September 26, 1872 ($978); Ste. Genevieve on May 27, 1873 ($3,500); Gads Hill on January 31, 1874 ($2,000); Otterville on July 7, 1876 ($15,000); Glendale on October 8, 1879 ($6,000); Winston on July 15, 1881 ($4,000); and Blue Cut on September 7, 1881 ($16,000).

Jesse and Frank James were often blamed for robberies they claimed they did not do. Some of these robberies were likely done by copycat robbers and former James Gang members in concert with others.

Jesse James was said to have been a member of the secret organization known collectively as the Knights of the Golden Circle. This group was formed from many other groups organized to protect southern rights, expand slavery and create an independent country that could include other countries

Confederate guerrilla Jesse James, armed with three pistols, in 1864. He had already killed many men in the Civil War. *Missouri Historical Society.*

in or around the Gulf of Mexico and the Caribbean. Legends claim that treasures set aside to create this new country after the Civil War were hidden in Arkansas, Kansas, Missouri, Oklahoma and elsewhere.

Outlaw Cole Younger and his brothers Jim, John and Bob were often part of the James-Younger Gang. The Younger brothers were believed to have taken part in robberies in Kansas, Kentucky, Missouri and West Virginia. The brothers were part of the ill-fated attempt with the James brothers to rob banks in Northfield, Minnesota.

The Northfield raid party consisted of the James-Younger Gang of eight outlaws: Jesse James, Frank James, Bob Younger, Jim Younger, Cole Younger, Clell (McClellan) Miller, Samuel Wells (alias Charlie Bitts) and Bill Stiles (alias Bill Chadwell). The gang attempted to rob the First National Bank of Northfield on September 21, 1876. The town's citizens were alerted and attacked the robbers. Two citizens were murdered by the outlaws. Two outlaws were killed. With the new telegraph system, towns and lawmen in the area were alerted, and as many as five hundred citizens and lawmen traveled in a number of posses to track down the gang and keep them from escaping Minnesota. The gang split up. All of the Younger brothers were wounded in a gunfight on September 21 and were captured by a posse of at least seven men at Medelia, Minnesota. The Youngers were sent to prison and were almost lynched. Another outlaw from the Northfield robbery was killed later. Jesse and Frank James managed to escape, but the James-Younger Gang was no more. Any loot some of its members had hidden in Missouri might still be unrecovered.

On April 3, 1882, Robert Ford murdered Jesse James in St. Joseph, Missouri, while James was on a chair straightening a crooked picture on his wall. Ford claimed a $10,000 reward but was paid only a small portion of it. Frank James was a fugitive for many years. He negotiated terms of his surrender to authorities and was tried for only a few of the robberies he committed as well as a murder in Missouri. Due to a combination of politics, Reconstruction animosities and legal tricks, Frank James was able to avoid conviction and spent no time in prison, other than when he was jailed

Charles Fletcher Taylor, Jesse James and Frank James were Confederate guerrillas. The James brothers became robbers after the Civil War. *Missouri Historical Society*.

This scene, called "Jesse James Reception," is indicative of the novels and stories crafted about him and his gang. *Library of Congress.*

several times to be tried. Frank bought a farm near Fletcher, Oklahoma, and reportedly recovered several caches belonging to the James Gang, but not all of them.

Outlaw loot was often buried or hidden after a robbery, as gold and silver coins were heavy and posses were usually formed quickly. After a robbery, outlaws would generally split up the loot, with each robber going in a different direction to confuse a posse. Outlaws usually had faster horses than members of a posse and would stake fresh horses along their escape routes in order to outpace the posse. Individual outlaws seemed to often hide a number of small caches of loot to draw on over time when they were traveling and out of cash.

Stories about outlaws are hard to research, as these men lied repeatedly and used aliases to hide their identities. Their families, friends and fellow gang members also lied repeatedly under oath to keep the criminal out of jail or away from the hangman's noose.

Over time, outlaws became known as gangsters. Loot from their illegal actions were said to be in the St. Louis and Kansas City areas, where the mobs were based. About $300,000 in cash related to the Greenlease kidnapping in 1953 is still unaccounted for.

Outlaw loot caches include the following: Berry's Loot, Andrew County; Tin Whistle Loot, Barton County; Cole Younger Cache, Cass County; Liberty Bank Robbery Loot, Clay County; Winston Railroad Robbery Loot, Daviess County, Clinton County and DeKalb County; Jesse James Blue

Bob, James, Cole Younger and their mother are shown here. As a result of their participation in the James-Younger Gang, the brothers went to prison. *Historical Society of Missouri.*

Bob Ford murdered Jesse James in St. Joseph. James's murder sealed his lips about any caches only he knew about. *Library of Congress.*

Spring Loot, Jackson County; Cole Younger Alba Cache, Jasper County; Kansas City Southern Robbery Loot, Jasper County; Farrington Treasure, Lawrence County; Jesse James Cache, Ozark County; Lost Possum Lodge Treasure; Pulaski County; James Gang Cache, St. Clair County; Gangster Jewelry Cache, St. Louis County; Greenlease Kidnapping Ransom, St. Louis County; Gangster Treasure, Sullivan County; Outlaw Lookout Tower Treasure, Texas County; and Jesse James Gads Hill Loot, Wayne County.

7

TREASURE CAVES

Missouri has more than six thousand known caves, and many of them have been used by Indians and others over the years. Most of these caves are in the Ozarks, which covers much of southern Missouri. Missouri caves are found in limestone and dolostone rocks where, over hundreds of thousands to millions of years, rainwater seeped into the ground and dissolved carbonate rock along fractures, cracks, joints and through permeable rock. Over time, the carbonate rocks were eroded and water absorbed the minerals. Sometimes these minerals were deposited in caves as stalactites and stalagmites that can be seen today. Many caves had underground pools of water and held rivers of water that flowed to the surface out of springs. Springs are everywhere in the Ozarks. When water tables dropped due to changes in topography, uplifts, weather changes or human intervention (wells and dams, for example), these caves become accessible from the surface. Some Missouri caves are full of water and are seldom explored, as cave diving is very hazardous.

Since caves have a fairly constant temperature and provide protection from storms, cold, heat and predators, they have been inhabited for centuries. Indians, settlers, Civil War guerrillas, outlaws and others have lived in them or have taken refuge in them. Some caves are actually bluff shelters caused by harder rock overlaying softer rock that has been eroded in part by wind and water over time. Bluff shelters are often located along rivers and streams. They may be located higher up on the sides of valleys, as water courses may have eroded deep into rock and caused incised valleys over time.

Many Missouri caves like this one were rumored to have treasure hidden in them. *State Historical Society of Missouri.*

Inside the Mark Twain Cave, where legends claim treasure was hidden. *State Historical Society of Missouri.*

I have sought treasure in a few caves in Stoddard County, Missouri, with my metal detector, without success. Many caves have just solid rock and evaporite deposits in them, making it hard for treasure to be hidden there. Where soil deposits or rock debris from cave collapses exist, treasure can be hidden under this material.

I suspect that some of the treasure stories associated with commercial caves might be public-relations ploys to attract tourists. Everyone wants to find a lost treasure in a cave. Many Missouri caves are not well known but have lost treasure stories associated with them. Sometimes, it is easy to miss a small cave's entrance, as it might be covered by vegetation or fallen rocks. Sinkholes are caves that have collapsed and are indications of large cave complexes in an area.

Caves with treasure stories include the following: Rockhouse Cave, Barry County; Sugar Silver Cave, Barry County; Tim Whistle Loot, Barton County; Migrating Indians Cache, Benton County; Money Cave, Dent County; Bushwhackers Loot, Howell County; Mark Twain Cave Treasures, Marion County; Ramsey Cave, Miller County; Bruce Cave, Moniteau County; Ground Creek Cave, Phelps County; Madre Vena Cave Treasure, McDonald County; Ozark Wonder Cave, McDonald County; Spanish Miners Bear Hollow Gold, McDonald County; Carroll's Cave, Shannon County; Lost Silver Cave, St. Clair County; Old Lost Alonzus Hall Treasure, Stone County; Parson Keithy's Gold, Stone County; Spanish Cave Treasure, Stone County; Alf Bolin's Treasure, Taney County; Licking Treasure, Texas County; William Silvey Treasure, Washington County; and Spanish Cave Treasure, Wright County.

8

SHIPWRECKS

The Missouri River was a major transportation route from St. Louis to the West. Steamboats traveled as far upstream as central Montana and the Montana gold fields. The Mississippi River serves as the eastern boundary for the state of Missouri and was the major inland route of U.S. trade. Along these waterways are more than four hundred steamboat shipwrecks within the state of Missouri or adjacent to its boundaries with Illinois and Kansas.

Due to the large number of shipwrecks, the United States began to invest in snagging and channel stabilization with rocked banks to reduce navigation hazards. The Missouri and Mississippi Rivers have channels that have meandered over the last several centuries and since Americans have used these rivers for transportation.

Shipwrecks were a navigation hazard in the Mississippi and Missouri Rivers. The U.S. Army Corps of Engineers and Missouri River Commission's *Annual Reports of the War Department for the Fiscal Year Ended June 30, 1897, Report of the Chief of Engineers* listed 295 shipwrecks on the Missouri River. The primary causes of these shipwrecks were snags (193), fire (25), ice (26), rocks (11) and bridges (10). Other reasons for shipwrecks were boiler explosions, storms and wind, sandbars, collisions, overloading and swamping. Most of the shipwrecks tabulated by the U.S. Army in this report were in the state of Missouri. The data on the shipwrecks was collected from reliable sources, including St. Louis newspapers and the St. Louis Merchants Exchange.

The steamboats *Spread Eagle* and *Dubuque*, seen here at St. Louis, were typical of large vessels on the Mississippi River. *Library of Congress.*

The first thirty years of steamboat commerce on the Missouri, Mississippi and Ohio Rivers saw 233 steamboat shipwrecks with 1,015 killed and 1,805 injured, according to a tabulation from 1848. Shipwrecks from 1819 to 1880s were listed in William M. Lytle and Forest R. Holdcamper's book *Merchant Steam Vessels of the United States: 1790–1868* (Steamship Society of America). But the book is missing a number of shipwrecks that occurred in the Missouri and Mississippi Rivers. Lists of steamship wrecks give general locations to the nearest town or landmark. Some of these towns and landmarks no longer exist. Island No. 10 near New Madrid washed away after the Civil War and exists no more. Many shipwrecks are under dry to soggy land in floodways that are part of flood-control systems managed by the U.S. Army Corps of Engineers. The Corps of Engineers was given the mission to improve navigation, reduce risk and minimize flooding as much as possible. The United States spent millions of dollars over more than a century to make navigation safer and faster by pulling out snags and channeling water to form fewer bends, which caused the river's flow speeds to increase.

In spite of the large number of shipwrecks, few people died in these incidents. Most steamboats were sunk by snags and often in relatively shallow water not far from land. There were also a lot of other steamboats and other boats navigating the rivers, so help was usually nearby. Loss of

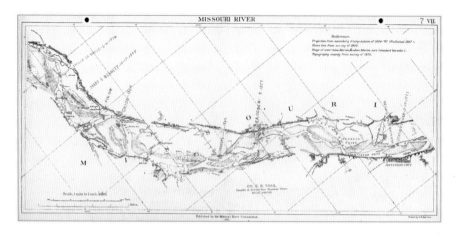

A map showing the location of eight shipwrecks upstream from Jefferson City. *State Historical Society of Missouri.*

life generally occurred from ship collisions and boilers exploding. Salvage of parts of cargo and treasure was more likely with steamers that sank in shallow water or near shore. Often, a wrecked ship had much of its superstructure and chimneys above water to mark its location. The upper decks of a sunken steamer would sometimes be carried off from the wreck and float downstream due to snags hitting the ship and the force of the current. Due to the high silt content in the Missouri and Mississippi Rivers, if salvage did not begin quickly, the parts of the vessel underwater would silt up. Sunken steamboats often caused changes in the river; meandering rivers often left steamboats under land in a few years.

Most of the vessels and their cargo were covered by insurance companies. These companies often commissioned boats to salvage sunken vessels' cargo and equipment. The most valuable part of a steamboat was its engine. If possible, an engine was removed and put onto another steamboat.

Steamboat cargos varied. Farm products such as corn, wheat, tobacco and lumber would go downstream. Merchant supplies, migrants and their supplies and money for soldiers and U.S. government staff went upstream. Some steamships carried mixed cargo and passengers. Passengers would likely have carried money for their trips or for trading. Before the Civil War, funds would generally be in silver and gold coins, although bank notes and currency would also be used for commercial transactions. After the war, currency and bank notes were carried for large sums aboard ships. Since there were few deaths on shipwrecks, it is likely that most passengers and crew escaped with their money. Trunks containing valuables were often left behind. A safe for a steamer's use to buy fuel and other items would be on board, and it might store funds belonging to passengers and others. Most likely, the purser or captain would empty the safe before abandoning the shipwreck.

One passenger on the steamer *Buford* had $6,000 in specie in his trunk, which was lost on April 25, 1840, after the *Buford* hit a snag and sank in about one minute near the mouth of the Missouri River. For treasure to be lost, a ship had to sink quickly. When ships sank in deep water, recovery was rare.

Gold was sometimes shipped from the Montana gold fields after the discovery of the precious metal there in 1858. The opening of other gold fields followed in 1862 and later. Explosions and fires that destroyed steamers are likely to have left behind unsalvageable cargo and treasure. Since the steamer *Ruth* had $2.6 million in Union currency on board when it was set afire and sank, the U.S. government hired divers and salvage experts. They raised what they could and then blew up the wreck with gunpowder.

Although the steamboat *Arabia* sank in Wyandotte County, Kansas, on September 5, 1856, in only two minutes after hitting a walnut tree snag in the Missouri River, it is representative of Missouri shipwrecks and what they might contain. This wreck is close to the Missouri state line. The Hawley family and their friends in 1988 and 1989 found and salvaged the shipwreck under a cornfield about one-half mile from the current Missouri River channel. They excavated around the wreck and used powerful pumps to drop the water level so they could recover much of the two hundred tons of cargo of clothes, china, dishes, guns, tools and other items heading upriver from its last stop at Westport Landing in what is now Kansas City. The recovered cargo was put on display in the *Arabia* Steamboat Museum in Kansas City. Prior to the successful complete salvage of the *Arabia*'s cargo by Greg Hawley and his family and friends, salvage attempts had been made in 1877, 1897 and 1975 without much success. Any whiskey on board the *Arabia* must have been salvaged right after its sinking or floated off the wreck. Several books mention a steamer called the *Francis X. Aubrey* sinking at the location of the *Arabia*. I could find no historical evidence of the *Francis X. Aubrey* sinking there, but that was the name of a steamboat. I think that name instead of the *Arabia* was used mistakenly in a source. Francis X. Aubrey was a trader and freighter, so it is likely that the whiskey and freight on the *Arabia* was his, thus causing confusion over time.

Another representative of excavated Missouri River steamboats is the *Bertrand*. The *Bertrand* was a 251-ton stern-wheel steamer. It was 161 feet

A large snag sinking the *Bertrand* in the Missouri River. Most shipwrecks were caused by snags. *State Historical Society of Missouri.*

long with a beam of 32 feet, 9 inches; a depth of 5 feet, 2 inches; and a light draft of 1 foot, 6 inches. It was built in 1864 at Wheeling, West Virginia, and carried engines and machinery salvaged from the shipwrecked *A.J. Sweeney.* It was steaming up the Missouri River with supplies for the new Montana Territory mining districts. It carried a very valuable cargo of food, five thousand barrels of whiskey, clothes, agricultural goods, mining supplies, more than one hundred earthenware carboys of mercury, machinery and ammunition for U.S. Army twelve-pounder howitzers.

The *Bertrand* was snagged on April 1, 1865, and sank in five to ten minutes in eight feet of water near present-day Blair, Nebraska, in De Soto Bend of the Missouri River. The location is in what is now the De Soto National Wildlife Refuge. The boat was insured. Within six weeks of it sinking, most of the valuable machinery, mercury and whiskey had been salvaged. Another sunken steamer, the *Cora II*, was salvaged several hundred feet upstream of the wreck of the *Bertrand*. In 1968, the *Bertrand* was found by Jesse Pursell and Sam Corbino with a magnetometer. They salvaged the *Bertrand* from 1968 to 1969 on U.S. government land in a wildlife refuge. The contract gave 60 percent of the salvaged material to the U.S. government and 40 percent to the salvagers. Over one million items and nine carboys of mercury were recovered from the shipwrecked *Bertrand*. The vessel was buried under twenty-seven feet of silt and sand and required pumps and heavy equipment to salvage. The U.S. Fish and Wildlife's De Soto National Wildlife Refuge has a museum that displays recovered history from the *Bertrand*. After recovery, the hull and remains of the wreck were covered with fill. The wreck is listed in the National Register of Historic Places.

Another Missouri River sunken steamboat that was salvaged was the *Twilight*, in 2001. Much of its cargo had been removed previously, especially during an 1897 salvage. Other steamboats have likely been found and possibly salvaged in part in recent years.

A large number of steamboats were lost in the St. Louis area, especially due to ice and fires when steamboats were packed into the St. Louis landing area. In 1856, the breakup of ice on the Mississippi River caused ice to pile up on the moored steamers. The *Submarine No. 4* (a salvage ship) capsized and sank. At least seven steamboats were torn from their moorings by the ice and floated downstream with the ice flow. Two steamboats were sunk by collision with other boats and with a floating wharf during an ice flow.

During the massive St. Louis fire of May 17, 1849, twenty-three steamboats, three barges and many small boats tied up on the landing were destroyed by flames, along with much of downtown. During the Civil War,

Mississippi River steamboats are seen close together. Sinking from collisions was common. *State Historical Society of Missouri.*

Island No. 10 Confederate shipwrecks in the Mississippi River. Many steamboats were sunk during the Civil War. *U.S. Navy.*

Confederate agents set a fire on July 5, 1863, which burned up the Union steamers *Cherokee*, *Edward F. Dix*, *Glasgow*, *Northerner*, *Sunshine* and *Welcome*. On September 13, 1863, Confederate agents set another fire along the St. Louis landing. The blaze destroyed the *Imperial*, *Hiawatha*, *Jesse K. Bell* and *Post Boy*.

Many sunken steamboats were salvaged shortly after they sank. Sometimes, they were almost completely salvaged of their cargo. Before dams were built upstream, water flows varied greatly seasonally, so a ship sunk during high water in the spring might be almost completely out of the water at the end of the summer. Professional salvage boats were used on the Missouri and Mississippi Rivers. Sometimes, snag boats from the U.S. Army Corps of Engineers and boats under contract to the U.S. government removed shipwrecks that were hazards to navigation. In 1889–90, the U.S. Army Corps of Engineers removed three shipwrecks in the Osage River. Over the years, many people have searched for shipwrecks.

BIBLIOGRAPHY

GOVERNMENT DOCUMENTS

Annual Reports of the War Department for the Fiscal Year Ended June 30, 1897, Report of the Chief of Engineers. Washington, D.C.: Government Printing Office, 1897.

Mineral and Water Resources of Missouri, Report of the United States Geological Survey and Missouri Division of Geological Survey and Water Resources. Washington, D.C.: U.S. Government Printing Office, 1967.

Official Records of the Union and Confederate Navies in the War of the Rebellion. 30 vols. Washington, D.C.: Government Printing Office, 1894–1922.

Report of the Chief of Engineers Accompanying Report of the Secretary of War, 1867. Washington, D.C.: Government Printing Office, 1867.

Report of the Chief of Engineers Accompanying Report of the Secretary of War, 1868. Washington, D.C.: Government Printing Office, 1869.

Slave Narratives: A Folk History of Slavery in the United States from Interviews with Former Slaves, Typewritten Records Prepared by the Federal Writers' Project, 1936–1938, Assembled by the Library of Congress Project. Vol. 10. Washington, D.C.: Works Progress Administration for the District of Congress, 1941.

U.S. Department of the Navy, Civil War Chronology: 1861–1865. Washington, D.C.: Government Printing Office, 1971.

The War of the Rebellion: A Compilation of the Official Records of the Union and Confederate Armies. 128 vols. Washington, D.C.: Government Printing Office, 1880–1901.

Wharton, Hayward, M., James A. Martin, Adrel W. Rueff, Charles E. Robertson, Jack S. Wells and Eva B. Kisraranyul. *Missouri Minerals Resources, Production and Forecasts.* Rolla: Missouri Geological Survey and Water Resources, 1969.

Williams, Dr. Charles P. *Industrial Report on Lead, Zinc, and Iron Together with Notes on Shannon County and Its Copper Deposits.* Geological Survey of Missouri. Jefferson City, MO: Regan & Carter, State Printers & Binders, 1877.

BIBLIOGRAPHY

NEWSPAPERS

Daily Illinois State Journal (Springfield, IL), August 6 and 8, 1863.
Niles Register (Baltimore, MD), June 20, 1840.

BOOKS

Bass, George F., ed. *Ships and Shipwrecks of the Americas: A History Based on Underwater Archaeology*. New York: Thames and Hudson, 1988.

Batels, Carolyn M. *Civil War Stories of Missouri*. Independence, MO: Two Trails Publishing, 1994.

Breihan, Carl W. *The Killer Legions of Quantrill*. Seattle, WA: Superior Publishing Company, 1971.

———. *Quantrill and His Civil War Guerillas*. Denver, CO: Sage Books, 1959.

Cottrell, Steve. *The Battle of Carthage and Carthage in the Civil War*. Carthage, MO: City of Carthage, 1990.

Drago, Harry Sinclair. *The Steamboaters: From the Early Side-Wheelers to the Big Packets*. New York: Bramhall House, 1967.

Dyer, Frederick H. *A Compendium of the War of the Rebellion*. Des Moines, IA: Dyer Publishing Company, 1908.

Fellman, Michael. *Inside War: The Guerilla Conflict in Missouri during the American Civil War*. New York: Oxford University Press, 1989.

Foley, William E., and C. David Rice. *The First Chouteaus: River Barons of Early St. Louis*. Urbana: University of Illinois Press, 1983.

Forister, Robert H. *Bloomfield, Missouri, Highland in the Swamps*. Bloomfield, MO: Robert H. Forister, 2003.

Gaines, W. Craig. *Civil War Gold and Other Lost Treasure*. Rev. ed. N.p.: Amazon KDP, 2017.

———. *Hispanic Treasure of the Eastern United States*. N.p.: Amazon KDP, 2021.

Getler, Warren, and Bob Brewer. *Rebel Gold: One Man's Quest to Crack the Code Behind the Secret Treasure of the Confederacy*. New York: Simon & Schuster, New York, 2003.

Gibson, Arrell M. *Wilderness Bonanza: The Tri-State District of Missouri, Kansas, and Oklahoma*. Norman: University of Oklahoma Press, 1972.

Hawley, Greg. *Treasure in a Cornfield: The Discovery and Excavation of the Steamboat Arabia*. Kansas City, MO: Paddle Wheel Publishing, 1998.

Heidenry, John. *Zero at the Bone*. New York: St. Martin's Press, 2009.

Henson, Michael Paul. *America's Lost Treasures*. South Bend, IN: Jayco Publishing, 1984.

Ingenthron, Elmo. *Borderland Rebellion: A History of the Civil War on the Missouri-Arkansas Border*. Branson, MO: Ozarks Mountaineer, 1980.

Jameson, W.C. *Buried Treasures of the Ozarks*. Little Rock, AR: August House Publishers, 1990.

———. *Lost Mines and Buried Treasures of Missouri*. Henderson, TN: Goldminds Publishing, 2011.

Kemp, James Furman. *The Ore Deposits of the United States and Canada*. New York: Engineering and Mining Journal, 1905.

Lytle, William M., and Forest R. Holdcamper. *Merchant Steam Vessels of the United States: 1790–1868*. Warwick, RI: Steamship Historical Society of America, 1975.

Marx, Robert F. *Buried Treasure of the United States, How and Where to Locate Hidden Wealth*. New York: Bonanza Books, 1978.

McReynolds, Edwin C. *Missouri: A History of the Crossroads State*. Norman: University of Oklahoma Press, 1975.

Monaghan, Jay. *Civil War on the Western Border, 1854–1865*. New York: Bonanza Books, 1956.

Patterson, Richard. *Historical Atlas of the Outlaw West*. Boulder, CO: Johnson Books, 1993.

Penfield, Thomas. *Buried Treasure in the U.S. and Where To Find It*. New York: Grosset & Dunlap, 1969.

———. *A Guide to Treasure in Missouri*. Conroe, TX: True Treasure Publishers, 1976.

Peterson, Paul R. *Quantrill in Texas: The Forgotten Campaign*. Nashville, TN: Cumberland House, 2007.

Rafferty, Milton D. *Historical Atlas of Missouri*. Norman: University of Oklahoma Press, 1981.

Schoolcraft, Henry R. *A View of the Lead Mines of Missouri*. New York: Charles Wiley & Company, 1819.

Schurmacher, Emile C. *Lost Treasures and How to Find Them!* New York: Paperback Library, 1968.

Settle, William A., Jr. *Jesse James Was His Name*. Lincoln: University of Nebraska Press, Bison Books, 1977.

Simmons, Mark. *Murder on the Santa Fe Trail: An International Incident, 1843*. El Paso: Texas Western Press, 1987.

Starr, Stephen Z. *Jennison's Jayhawkers, A Civil War Cavalry Regiment and Its Commander*. Baton Rouge: Louisiana State University Press, 1973.

Steele, Phillip W. *Ozark Tales and Superstitions*. Gretna, LA: Pelican Publishing, 1983.

Tatham, Robert L. *Missouri Treasures and Civil War Sites*. Boulder, CO: H. Glenn Carson Enterprises, 1974.

Terry, Thomas P. *United States Treasure Map Atlas*. La Crosse, WI: Specialty Publishing, 1981.

Triplett, Frank. *The Life, Times & Treacherous Death of Jesse James*. Reprint of 1882 edition. N.p.: Longmeadow Press, 1992.

Walthall, John A. *Galena and Aboriginal Trade in Eastern North America*. Illinois State Museum, Scientific Papers. Vol. 17. Springfield, Illinois, 1981.

Weaver, H. Dwight, and Paul A. Johnson. *Missouri: The Cave State*. Jefferson City, MO: Discovery Enterprises, 1980.

Wood, Larry. *Other Noted Guerillas of the Civil War in Missouri*. Joplin, MO: Hickory Press, 2007.

ARTICLES

Artifact. "Lost Mines of Arkansas, Missouri." Vol. 2, no. 1 (February–March 1967): 11–13.

Bailey, Tom. "Mystery of the Lost Ozarks Silver." *Gold!* 3, no. 1 (Annual 1971): 14–15, 46.

Beights, Ronald. "Jesse James and the Gads Hill Train Holdup." *Wild West* (June 2005). Accessed in www.historynet.com.

Boren, Kerry Ross. "Arkansas's Spanish Treasure Cave." *Treasure World* 8, no. 7 (February–March 1974): 13–14.

Breihan, Carl W. "Find Shephard's $250,000 Rattlesnake Loot." *Treasure* 16, no. 3 (April 1979): 50–55, 57.

Brewington, G.H. "Phantom Message from Cayuga Springs." *True West* 16, no. 2 (November–December 1968): 22–23, 46–48.

Gaines, Jay R. "The $1,000,000 Madre Vena Treasure." *Treasure* 9, no. 4, 26–29, 72.

Gaines, W. Craig. "Alf Bolin's Lost Loot." *Treasure Cache* (2017): 40–41.

———. "Knights of the Golden Circle Treasure." *Lost Treasure* 38, no. 9 (September 2013): 18–19.

———. "Lost Ozark Mines." *Lost Treasure* 41, no. 2 (April 2016): 9–10.

———. "Mississippi Mud." *Lost Treasure* 24, no. 4 (April 1999): 18–19.

———. "Research Unravels Mystery of Slater's Mine." *Treasure Search* 14, no. 6 (November–December 1986): 38–39, 41.

Gibbons, Robert H. "Lost Spanish Gold in a Missouri Cave." *Treasure World* 5, no. 11 (October–November 1971): 30–32, 34–36.

Haydon, Glenn E. "Sunken Treasure Every Five Miles." *Saga* 36, no. 6 (September 1968): 20–21, 58, 60–62.

Henson, Michael Paul. "Vast Hidden Wealth Still Awaits Discovery in 'Show Me' State." *Lost Treasure* 8, no. 6 (June 1983): 30–35.

Hoots, Carl F. "Bushwhacker Treasure." *Treasure World* 6, no. 9 (August–September 1971): 30–32, 34–35.

Kelly, Bill. "6 Year Old Kidnapped, Recover the Greenlease Ransome Loot." *Treasure Cache* (2000): 10–12.

Kivett, Gene. "Missing Nail Keg of Gold Coins." *True Treasure* 5, no. 8 (July–August 1971): 25–27.

Klein, Frederick S. "The Sinking of the *Ruth.*" *Civil War Times Illustrated* 1, no. 4 (July 1975): 48–49.

Lowry, Mike. "Treasures of the Big Muddy." *True Treasure* 4 no. 1 (January–February 1970): 49–50.

McGowan, Bob H. "Missouri's Possible Fortune in Silver." *True West* 17 no. 2 (December 1969): 43, 58–60.

Meis, Joe. "Famous Kidnapping Ransom Money Missing." *Treasure Cache* (2006 Annual): 30–32.

Murrell, John. "Guerilla Caches." *Lost Treasure* 29, no. 4 (April 2004): 8–10.

———. "Where Is Jim Berry's Loot." *Treasure Cache* (2003 Annual): 30–32.

Pallante Anthony J. "Missouri General Order No. 11." *Lost Treasure* 25, no. 12 (December 2000): 43–45.

Penfield, Tom. "True Treasure Answers Your Questions." *True Treasure* 6, no. 10 (September–October 1972): 56, 58.

Rother, Charlotte. "Missouri's Lost Spanish Gold." *Lost Treasure* 2, no. 7 (June 1977), 54, 56.

Tisserand, Jacques, and Hack Barnes. "Missouri's Lost Copper Mine." *True Treasure* 5 no. 10 (September–October 1971): 31.

Todd, Leora Coffin. "Mystery of the Lost Ozarks Silver." *Gold!* 3, no. 1 (1971 Annual): 17, 32.

Toothman, Rick. "The Pitfalls of Looking for Outlaw Gold." *Western Treasures* 4, no. 1 (October 1968): 24–25.

Townsend, Ben. "Missouri's Missing $10,000 Gold Caches." *True Treasure* 8, no. 4 (March–April 1974): 11–12.

———. "Missouri's Spanish Treasure Trove," *Lost Treasure* 1, no. 8 (July 1976): 22–25.

———. "Missouri Trove the Forty-Niners Missed," *Treasure* 5, no. 12 (December 1974): 59–67, 76.

Treasure Search. "Fabulous Missouri Gold Coin Cache." Vol. 10, no. 6 (December 1982): 14–15.

Villa, Benito. "The Preacher's Lost Gold," *Treasure World* 8, no. 11 (October–November 1974): 57–58.

Western Treasures. "Gold in Neosho." Vol. 6, no. 5 (December 1972): 20–25, 66.

Wolford-Perry, Janet. "De Soto in Missouri?" *Lost Treasure* 28, no. 4 (April 2003): 31–33.

Websites

Cathedral of the Immaculate Conception. www.kcgolddome.org.

Civil War on the Western Border. Kansas City Public Library. www.civilwaronthewesternborder.org.

Community & Conflict: The Impact of the Civil War in the Ozarks. www.ozarkscivilwar.org.

Federal Bureau of Investigation. www.fbi.gov.

Legends of America. www.legendsofamerica.com.

Wikipedia. www.wikipedia.org.

ABOUT THE AUTHOR

W. Craig Gaines is the author or coauthor of *Hispanic Treasures of the Eastern United States*; *Hispanic Treasures of the Western United States*; *The Confederate Cherokees, John Drew's Regiment of Mounted Rifles*; *Encyclopedia of Civil War Shipwrecks*; *Civil War Gold and Other Lost Treasures*; *Success in Life*; *Nostradamus' Curse*; *Great Lost Treasure Never Found*; as well as other books and articles. The History Press has published his *Lost Oklahoma Treasure*, *Lost Texas Treasure* and *Lost California Treasure*. Craig has been interested in lost treasure since seeing the film *Treasure Island* when he was very young. He has written lost treasure stories for a variety of treasure hunting magazines over the years. Craig is an engineer, geologist and writer who has been in many of the areas mentioned in this book. He and his wife live in Tulsa, Oklahoma.

The author as a five-year-old cowboy. *Author collection.*